Averse Again Now and Then

To Scott & Trida - Your library is always better when it has the disguise of literature. My best, always! Tommy

Averse Again Now and Then

– LIGHT VERSE FROM THE PLUFF MUD POET –

W. Thomas McQueeney

Cover Photo by Author: Brilliant sky at French Polynesian cove, 2006.

Painting comes from our 2006 trip to Bora Bora.

© 2017 W. Thomas McQueeney
McQueeney Creative, LLC
1105 Mazzy Lane
Mt. Pleasant, South Carolina 29464
All rights reserved.

ISBN: 154242156X
ISBN 13: 9781542421560

Dedication

It is with sincere appreciation and a most humble bow of acknowledgement that this volume is produced to honor those brilliant and dedicated professors who had guided me and others so many years ago. They were a most cohesive, entertaining, and demanding lot, the English Department at The Citadel in the early 1970's. They found places to interject Chaucer, Milton, Shakespeare, Fitzgerald, and Yeats into young minds who were discovering the world outside those imposing gates of demarcation at our military campus. We remember them as captains, majors, and colonels. In this volume, I recognize the devotion and mentorship of those legendary professors—James B. Carpenter, James A.W. Rembert, Malcolm M. Brennan, Samuel J. McCoy, D. Archie McDowell, Tony N. Redd, John R. Doyle, Richard J. Hansen, Kent Emery, Woody L. Holbein, Norman MacLeod, James M. O'Neill, John A. Riley, Louis Weile, Hugh O. Peurifoy, and W. Bland Mathis. A descriptive of the English Department written in the *1974 Sphinx* aptly suggests, "The emphasis is on the art of living rather than making a living."[1]

As Charles Dickens wrote, "I never could have done what I have done without the habits of punctuality, order, and diligence, without the determination to concentrate myself on one subject at a time."[2] Those professors from decades ago coerced and inspired. I salute them in gratitude.

Table of Contents

	Foreword · xiii	
	Introduction · xv	
Chapter 1	Get Up for a Resurrection · · · · · · · · · · · · · · · · · · 1	
	A Child of the Pluff Mud · · · · · · · · · · · · · · · · · · 3	
	Rhetoric Frederick · 4	
	Mascots of Abstract Thought · · · · · · · · · · · · · · · 5	
	Upon Presenting the Laurel · · · · · · · · · · · · · · · · 6	
	Swiss Clockolates · 7	
	Surely The Tapping Temple · · · · · · · · · · · · · · · · 9	
	Much Amiss · 12	
	Yikes! Dating Sites! · 14	
	Doggone It · 15	
	Residential Style · 16	
	The Cliché Bouquet · 17	
Chapter 2	What's a Bird in the Bush Worth? · · · · · · · · · · · · 19	
	Courtship Journey · 21	
	Kells · 22	
	A Limerick Limerick · 22	
	Query in a Quarry · 23	
	The Fall of Spring Training · · · · · · · · · · · · · · · 25	
	Near the Outlet of an Inlet · · · · · · · · · · · · · · · 26	
	Yeti Still Has Nightmares · · · · · · · · · · · · · · · · · 28	

	There's No *O* in Edinburgh	30
	LY¢PL8s	31
	Must Stash	33
Chapter 3	Making Sense of Where and Whence	35
	Know Your Phobia	37
	Nurse Eerie Verse	39
	Magic-Carpet Stride	39
	Whacko Zack	41
	An Esoteric Sesquipedalian Epitaph	42
	Spelchekked	43
	Hiram on High	44
	John Dark	47
	The Manner of the Manor	49
	Love Of	51
	The Out-the-Door Commodore	53
	Chronologies of Other Times	54
Chapter 4	Coyotes and Foxes	55
	Laughing Rodrigo	57
	Ineffable Ed	59
	Do Not Go Mental, Brother!	60
	DD Sick	61
	Embrace Your Glacier	63
	His First Name Was Lloyd	65
	Declan Twomey	67
	Frogs and Turtles	69
	The Curious Case of Yimmy Jager	70
	Left unto Thyself	72
	Obits are the Pits	75
Chapter 5	More Stars, Same Stripes	77
	Breezes in the Treezes	79
	Aleut Aloof	80
	Arizonian	82
	New Mexicode	83

	Home of Roger Miller ·85
	Sense for Census ·87
	Suffering Suffrage ·89
	Hi-Dee-Ho ·90
	Anorexics on Diets ·91
	To Helena Hand Basket ·92
Chapter 6	West by Midwest Zest ·95
	The Preacher in Pierre, SD · · · · · · · · · · · · · · · · · ·97
	Big Fur Coat ·98
	Colorado ·99
	Omaha "Steaks" Claim for Baseball · · · · · · · · · · · ·100
	Economic Data from Nevada · · · · · · · · · · · · · · · ·102
	Leslie Down from the Holler · · · · · · · · · · · · · · · ·103
	Oh Kansas, My Kansas! · · · · · · · · · · · · · · · · · · ·104
	Spa or Salon in Oregon · · · · · · · · · · · · · · · · · · ·106
	Dale Köester ·107
	Brendan and Brandon ·109
Chapter 7	Growth of a Notion · 113
	A Response in Wisconsin · · · · · · · · · · · · · · · · · · 115
	When the Council Bluffs · · · · · · · · · · · · · · · · · · 116
	Texas Two-Step · 117
	The Ft. Lauderdale Splash · · · · · · · · · · · · · · · · · 118
	Albert Kahn · 119
	Shakespeare Comes to Walmart · · · · · · · · · · · · · · 121
	Mizurah! ·122
	No Maine Tribute Goes Unnoticed · · · · · · · · · · · ·123
	Alabama Ramble ·125
	Illini Line Item ·126
Chapter 8	Manifest Quest ·129
	Per Capita ·131
	The Ballad of the Caesar Salad · · · · · · · · · · · · · · ·132
	It's Safe to Try the Pralines · · · · · · · · · · · · · · · · ·133
	An Elegy from Dayton Going South · · · · · · · · · · · ·134

	Memphis 451 Miles	136
	Bluegrass and Green Skies	138
	Vermonters Like Who Haiku	139
	Dot the Eye in Island	141
	They Got It All	142
	No Thanks, Mr. Stuyvesant	143
Chapter 9	Declaration of Interdependence	145
	Poca-Honey	147
	Barnacle Geese and Bobwhites	148
	Fellows of the Palmettos	149
	Mixed Lexicon on the Eastern Shore	151
	Where *R* the R's?	153
	Connecticut at Night	156
	An Ode to Georgia	157
	Urban Crawl	160
	Kite Flying 101	161
	Delawares on You	162
	Decency, Descent, and DC	163
Chapter 10	Alpaca Llama and You Bring the Jaguar	167
	Hurts My Ears	169
	Social Media	171
	Nuptials Disrupted	173
	The Crematorium Comes to the Top	174
	Dove Story	175
	Judgment	177
	Frontier Fantasy	178
	Cemetery Signs	179
	The Boracle of Wi-Fi	180
	Owen Cohen	182
	Alpaca Llama and You Bring a Jaguar	183
	Empirical Balance	184
Chapter 11	Another Deity in Paradise	187
	Rumors	189
	Tuscarora Jack	189

To My Fudge Mental Friends	190
Mercy Margot	191
Meeting in a Tornado	192
No Luck Whatsoever	194
Ned Niblick	197
No One to Watch Over	199
Is WWW about Wrestling?	201
The Pacifist Pugilist	203
A Blithering Idiot	205
Chapter 12 Heretic, There a Tick	207
Penny Ann the Dreamer	209
Putting Lyrica to Lyrics	211
The Nexus of the Sixties	213
It's Not What You Think	215
Trending to a Genre	217
Two Irishmen	218
My Last Dutch Dress	220
Johnny Johnston	221
My Emoji Is LOL	223
Perspective in a Puddle	223
Abundant Conundrums	226
The Throne Drone	227
Beauty is an Imperfect Imposter	229
Ruminations	230
Artwork Notes	233
About the Author	235
Endnotes	237

Morning view of gazebos near Kingston, Jamaica, 2010

Foreword

Tommy McQueeney is a gifted and prolific writer. He approaches life like a vaudeville talent scout, eschewing rose-colored glasses and using a full palette to find meaning and humor in the very ordinary. Tommy treats words as Forrest Gump treats a box of chocolates; his love of language is contagious.

A Verse Again Now and Then would have been well received at the Algonquin Round Table.[3]

Patrick Michael Duffy
Noted humorist and friend of the author

Introduction

Competition for the semiprecious time of the "literary" consumer to enjoy something different is more evident in the digital world than past generations could ever have imagined. Fine authors shuffle in and out of the cyber consciousness with beneficial support mechanisms like Instagram, Twitter, Facebook, and LinkedIn. The hyper marketing of these productions has come to the fore as well. Numerous hawkish websites ensure the popularity of just about any publication…for a fee! Growing a "branding" opportunity out of my hometown of Charleston, South Carolina, will require nuances that may not have been invented by the time this is published. But it's coming! It may be that I am content with the completion aspect of the production itself, allowing that posterity may judge its efficacy. To me, it's good enough to know that I did it, I enjoyed doing it, and it's done before I'm done!

With this production, a set is complete. The first volume of 2016, *At First Averse and then Another* now has its bookend companion. *Averse Again Now and Then* is partly an overflow of the first volume and partly new additions. It is hoped that the reader finds an upswing in mood by simply reading through a few offerings herein. This is meant to be a happy turnoff from life's highway.

Nostalgia and melancholy have conspired. This book had an early foundation that simmered for a time like my dad's Sunday-afternoon spaghetti sauce.

As a young teen, my father introduced me to Ogden Nash. The light verse was both clever and enjoyable. I found other light-verse champions en route to my growth of appreciation for literary wit. These were the masters at the use of double-entendre, pun, and the surprise ending. Ogden Nash was both the primer and the template for an unconventional insight upon the sometimes-stuffy literary world. Eventually, I was introduced to the writings of e.e. cummings, Mark Twain, Dorothy Parker, Oscar Wilde, Alfred E. Housman, and the wry sayings of western humorist Will Rogers. I would be remiss should I not mention the influence of entertainment via the television celebrity wit Julius "Nipsey" Russell and the legendary country singer Roger Miller. Miller was a gifted songwriter who demonstrated an aptitude for comedic rhyme.

The job openings for happy people have been posted. Not enough have applied. The world sends us reasons for misery—by news accounts, by invoices, by health concerns, and by relationships gone sour. Do you still get a traditional newspaper? Sometimes it's best to read the cartoons and the sports section first, and then throw away the rest. The aforementioned Alfred E. Housman detailed this attitude best during World War I. In his volume *A Shropshire Lad*,[4] Housman foreshadowed misery, as one would best understand by preparing for the worst. We are all subject to taking lower dosages of familiar poisons in our daily interactions, like the never-ending horrific news stories that have numbed our consciousness. Housman felt it was essential to manage these poisons in small applications in order to achieve a happier and longer life.

Averse Again Now and Then

> There was a king reigned in the East:
> There, when kings will sit to feast,
> They get their fill before they think
> With poisoned meat and poisoned drink.
> He gathered all the springs to birth
> From the many-venomed earth;
> First a little, thence to more,
> He sampled all her killing store;
> And easy, smiling, seasoned sound,
> Sate the king when healths went round.
> They put arsenic in his meat
> And stared aghast to watch him eat;
> They poured strychnine in his cup
> And shook to see him drink it up:
> They shook, they stared as white's their shirt:
> Them it was their poison hurt.
> —I tell the tale that I heard told.
> Mithridates, he died old."[5]

(Excerpt from "Terrence, This Is Stupid Stuff,"
by Alfred E. Housman)

A poet can elicit the mood of doom—or one can just wait long enough to discover one's own sense of discord with our friend and imminent foe—time! I profoundly believe, much like the fine humorists who have passed before us, that life is for the living. There is a static need within humanity to engender a smile. A laugh is special. Our souls leap upon a giggle.

The entries here are not meant for a cohesive winding theme other than the theme of light-hearted contrivances. They are for eyes that sparkle and hearts that spring up in joy.

We can herald an assist for the progression of the cyber world for books on Kindle-like tablets. I like the weight of a book, but the electronic sources save the trees and certainly lighten the knapsack. Names of most persons herein—like Ned Niblick, Declan Twomey, and Owen Cohen—are spontaneously contrived, though some Internet phonebook somewhere would surely turn up a few similarities. They are lifted from thin air.

This format meanders from 131 productions on various subjects to include a fifty-poem "countdown" submission of descriptives. These are the fifty states of the United States in reverse order of their admission to the union. They start in chapter 5. As an avid traveler, I found a thrill in the decades-long completion of a dream—to visit all fifty states. Many personal observances were utilized to cite these special places in verse. It was a natural subject for me to develop. Besides, the amazing Ogden Nash (1902-71) had already claimed the animal kingdom.

To wit:

The Duck
By Ogden Nash

Behold the duck.
It does not cluck.
A cluck it lacks.
It quacks.
It is specially fond
Of a puddle or pond.
When it dines or sups,
It bottoms up.

Averse Again Now and Then

Nash was prodigious, having written nearly five hundred submissions of comic verse, published between 1931 and his death in 1971.[6] I have barely written half that. In my mind, Nash is the eminent legend in this genre.

Owing to post-graduate training in the art of form, I have added samples of nearly every poetic device prescribed by the literary intellectuals of the past five hundred years. Even Haiku! Another villanelle, another sonnet, an ode, shape poems, and so forth, are rendered herein so that I was able to unload the guilt of not including them. Also included are a parody of a dramatic monologue, more limericks, and even an elegy. Mind you—within the ultimate goal of humor and entertainment—free verse rules best!

The world of highbrow literature will not notice this volume, nor will they ever know my name except in circles of instructions of "How Not To…" publish, write, paint, or entertain. *Acclaimed* and *Celebrated* will pass me by without even a glance. My soul's resolution within this enterprise was never for those reasons anyway. Likewise, it is that very same soul that holds my connection to my personal eternity and the simple concept of completion—knowing I wanted to accomplish the task for lesser reasons. That desire dates back to my maternal grandmother's inspiration and encouragement. The words from decades past appear with those dribblings of contemporary insight. A smirk to a smile is the triumph.

The artwork was used to weave pauses into the volume. All are original art productions also created by the author. Note that some guy named "Samôht" artistically signed a few. Yes, that's "Thomas" backwards. Early on, I endeavored to disguise my ineptitude in every art form. To be sure, none of the art has been on loan to national museums, iconic public buildings, or viable galleries.

As in the case of the first five books in publication, this compilation is also proceeds-directed to charitable and educational need. For this book, I have selected The Citadel Foundation Inc. The Citadel Foundation provides educational opportunities for young men and women in a military environment who seek the attainment of principled leadership within a world clamoring for its benefit. Personally, I owe much to this institution—its faculty, its alumni, and its impact upon my life for nearly a half century.

If there is a smile invoked, a perspective gained, a kindness offered, or a farce exposed…then this effort has attained the height of its intent. Never take yourself too seriously. I promise I will not fall into that chasm either. I hope that you will read your way into quiet contentedness on the way to happiness. It's the best place to be!

Averse Again Now and Then

South Carolina governor's mansion at Night, 2007

Chapter One

Get Up for a Resurrection

A Child of the Pluff Mud

That oily black upon my tracks
Wherever I trudge in that sludge,
And muck—once stuck on my boots—
Fiddler crabs and sweetgrass roots.
Tis the crime of grime for all time
From the Holy City's pluff mud bay.
It will never ever wash away.[7]

Rhetoric Frederick

Fred was an emergency substitute teacher
For sixth graders studying the world of rhetoric.
But the classroom full of precocious children
Had an overload of postulations awaiting Frederick.

"Is the sun only the sun in daytime?" they started.
"Why were two mosquitoes allowed onboard by Noah?
Why are outlaws always wanted, but in-laws are not?
Did they not see the crack that erupted Krakatoa?

"Would oceans be deeper if no sponges lived there?
Why do tugboats not tug boats, but push ships instead?
Why's the third hand on a watch the second hand?
If you get scared half to death twice, are you dead?"

"Slow down, children!" Fred formed his answer.
"Can a deaf person get a fair hearing in spite?
What disease was it that a 'cured ham' once had?
Why is night 'after dark' when it's really after light?"

The classroom was silent as he turned to the board
And began to list the conundrums in chalk.
The sixth grade classroom is a perfect place
Where society is singled out for its double-talk.

The one-time teacher had enlightened the class.
The children's questions were profoundly dramatic.
The principal never had Frederick back ever again—
He thought his postulations to be too pragmatic.

Mascots of Abstract Thought

The politically correct politically correctors
Counseled within the high school and college sectors.
'Twas there they found the shameful pursuits
Of teams named for Aztecs, Chippewas, and Utes.

Native American mascots, they said gave bad vibes
Like Red Raiders, Redskins, and other Indian tribes.
After the purge of Warriors, Seminoles, and Braves
They began assault on all team mascots making waves.

They termed religious monikers as intolerant names—
Those that had Crusaders and Cardinals playing in games.
And it didn't stop with Padres and Friars' team tags—
They had animus for animals like stallions and stags.

Being politically correct going politically forward—
Mascots will likely become unexcitable bore words.
Gender neutral, unbiased, and non-religious bureaucrats
Have declawed, spayed, and neutered even dogs and cats.

Upon Presenting the Laurel
In Thoughts and Words

Come hither, thy favorably anointed.
Though I am inwardly disappointed.
Kneel before the gilded sword.
Only I should be getting this award.
Accept this, thy dignified crest.
Though you are only second best.
I render ye this embroidered vestment.
By someone else's flawed assessment.
And pronounce to the world this glorious day.
I didn't want all that attention anyway.
That thy words are formed in fires of gold.
I hope you lose bladder control.
In every hamlet, and every city—
I blame the idiots on the committee.
Until death you'll hold this lofty honor.
You plagiarist, you pitiable phrase pawner!
Here's to you; I install this wreath.
Holding back anger, clenching my teeth.
For it is, to you, so richly earned.
My heart is weary, my stomach turned.
Let's stand with applause for our newest laureate.
My nemesis, my demon, my excoriate!
Then retire to the parlor and exchange lively toasts
With poisoned wine from bitter hosts.[8]

Swiss Clockolates

Amélie rode her bike to the marketplace
To gather her Alpine provisions.
She consulted the Swiss-born vendors there,
Confused by all the decisions.

The keepers spoke Italian, French, and German,
Some English and a little Romansch.
Her credit was fine with Diners Club,
Credit Suisse, Visa, or Carte Blanche.

Emmental, Camembert, or gruyère—
The robust cheese choices presented.
Helveticans have smelly traditions
In products notably fermented.

The Swiss are meticulously clever—
Neutrality means no wars are lost.
Yet they invented the Swiss Army knife—
With the irony of a Swiss flag embossed.

Omega, Rolex, or TAG Heuer?
Wristwatch, cuckoo, or grandfather?
Dark, milk, or white chocolate?
With almonds or raisins—why bother?

Amélie wanted fish from Lake Geneva—
Perch, ferà, pike, or trout?
Potato wheat, sourdough, or baguette?
What breads should she break out?

W. Thomas McQueeney

And wine should be complementary
To the supper she had planned.
Pinots, Chards, and Sauvignons—
Vintner's varieties of Switzerland!

Amélie pedaled home to her chalet
With just a sprig of grapes in her carrier.
Too much to decide in too little time!
If you want dinner with Amélie, marry her.

Surely The Tapping Temple
Make em Laugh!

Where Christopher Street crosses Greenwich[9]
And Puerto Ricans cajole each other in Spanish—
Where endless taxis form a yellow band
Around Manhattan's insular village land—
The redbrick building gathers paces now
From feet that know not why or how.
The best that ever was have danced away
Tapping in the timing of another day.

Singing in the rain like Gene Kelly
Or stepping out like Liza Minnelli,
Shake the sand dance like Mr. Bojangles,
Twirling on a boat and toeing the angles.
Gliding across fences was Fred Astaire
With Ginger Rogers atop her career.
Sammy Davis, Jr. had a walking cane prop,
As did Shirley Temple—her Good Ship Lollipop.

Tap became Gregory Hines's glorious epitaph—
And Donald O'Connor could really make em laugh.
Buddy Ebsen was a hoofer before he went lame;
Now he's in the International Tap Hall of Fame.
The studio gives lessons to little Manhattanites
Near the tap-dance enshrinements up two short flights.
It so very unfortunate for the store below
That Tap School lessons last an hour or so.

There's nothing so fashionable from the old Big Apple
As tophats, tuxedos, and orchestra'd tapple.
Back in the forties those rhythmic loafers
Earned highbrow praise and limousine chauffeurs.
Now tap is a dying art with very little revenue
Since the days of tap dancing have long bid adieu.
Still lessons are given daily on the second floor—
First-floor tenants long for the "old soft shoe" once more.

Averse Again Now and Then

Morris Island Lighthouse by water, 2005

Much Amiss

Find the moment to pause
And think "Egads!"
About the enormity of past popularities
And dying fads—
Like cargo pants, fallout shelters,
And boom boxes—
Beanie Babies, Slinkies,
And shoes called Crocses.
Gone are breakdancing
And the energetic Macarena,
MP3 players, Polaroids,
And news stories from Herzegovina.

Remember the old styles
Like mullet heads and the bandana?
Or stringed puka shells, lava lamps—
All classical Americana!
Whatever happened to long sideburns
Or the Rubik's Cube?
Or the turtleneck, the Walkman,
And the vacuum tube?
Tie-dyed shirts, platforms,
And Hula Hoops passed by.
Bellbottom jeans made fashion,
And no one asked why.

There used to be impractical fads
Like pet rocks,
Mood rings, Ouija boards,
And bobby socks.

Averse Again Now and Then

We had fun events like Trivial Pursuit
And paintball gaming.
They're gone to history—
Is the App Store worth blaming?
Ipods are Igone,
And so are flash mobs, too.
Atari, TiVo, and Pontiac
Have no more jobs for you.

No more eight-track players
Or even cassettes;
No Afros, no miniskirts,
Or disco duets—
Gone away today are
Cabbage Patch Dolls,
Tartan sweaters, leisure suits,
And overalls.
One can only hope that
Today's fads will die young—
Baggy pants, reality shows,
And piercings of the tongue.

Yikes! Dating Sites!

One would surely be predisposed
To date online without being disclosed.
If one is too shy for a date in person,
Try a dating site; it couldn't worsen.
They're everywhere and indiscreet
Want more kids? Try SingleParentMeet.
If it suits one better to start a batch,
There's another out there, PerfectMatch.
If you read the Bible and love a psalm,
Try this holy one—ChristianMingle.com
If you're more comfy in a synagogue,
There's a JDate site—start a Jewish blog.
Zoosk is popular, as is Plenty-of-Fish.
OKCupid could also get you your wish.
Chemistry dating is not for chemists.
It's more like eHarmony as its premise.
DateHookup and SpeedDate, likewise,
Will not get you out as fast as they advertise.
BlackPeopleMeet and SeniorPeopleMeet
Are not mutually exclusive, without deceit.
EliteSingles and ProfessionalMatch tend
To elevate the income levels of the blend.
OurTime and HowAboutWe breed plenty of clout,
Or just meet someone at work and ask em out.[10]

Doggone It

The children wanted an abandoned mutt,
Butt purebred lines were thought superior.
So we searched all canine types for sale,
From Afghans to the Yorkshire terrier.

Have you ever heard of a Xoloitzcuintli?
You can buy one from a breeder.
They came in mostly hairless varieties
For a grand with an automatic feeder.

One can purchase a two-toned Akita,
Or a Rottweiler or a Samoyed
For the price of a used pickup truck—
So these ones should be avoided.

A cute little King Charles Spaniel
Doesn't look like him at all.
They rate a nine-thousand-dollar price tag—
A risky investment for fetching a ball.

A Tibetan Mastiff puppy just sold
For a million dollars to a sheik.
This was a convincing enterprise.
We're going to the ASPCA next week.

Residential Style

Deborah and Ron went shopping for a home
Horribly undecided on the architectural style.
Ron was partial to Italianate or Cape Cod;
Deborah to Colonial or Spanish clay tile

The Dutch Colonial home they saw
Had no garage and a small back deck.
While the four-bedroom Art Deco model
Looked more like a Miami discotheque.

They couldn't tell the split-ranch home
From the Pueblo or the prairie.
They liked the color on the French Provincial,
But gasped at hints of contemporary.

Stately Georgian mansions were toured,
And a high-columned Greek Revival.
A small Queen Anne dollhouse they saw
Warmed Deb's house-hunting arrival.

But Ron was not thrilled by the trellises
And rejected Deborah's swooning.
He much preferred the Tudor estate
Where the hedges needed pruning.

A verbal volley and barrage ensued—
The couple was immersed in shellfire.
Deborah claimed her Regency birthright;
As Ron opted for the Second Empire.

The Cliché Bouquet

Try to avoid clichés like the plague,
And you'll never have to cry over spilt milk.
A cloud with silver lining is vague…
And the smoothest of smooth is not like silk.

Clichés arise because they foot the bill.
Time flies and when they rain, they pour.
Like someone who is dressed to kill—
Or finding anything fair in love and war.

All that glitters is not gold these days,
And acorns can fall far from a tree.
A witch hunt works in mysterious ways.
Why anyone ever beats the bushes beats me!

We bend over backward to make ends meet.
We should bite the bullet before biting the dust.
Why worry while there's a dead horse to beat.
Clichés go up and come down; they must!

The world's a stage and we are its players.
Clichés imply misunderstandings clear as a bell.
Stop the old wives' sayings by their newer purveyors,
By using original words—or go back to the well.

It's a necessary evil to make a long story short.
We should part company with clichés we ponder.
The whole ball of wax is in your court.
Their absence will make your heart grow fonder!

Alley view of St. Michael's Church steeple, Charleston, SC, 2005

Chapter Two

What's a Bird in the Bush Worth?

Courtship Journey

What gives value to a diamond?
The stone is quite resilient.
They are sparkly in daytime and
At nighttime, she'll find them brilliant.

What gives value to a black pearl?
They have deep organic luster.
A necklace ordered for your girl…
Don't buy it if you distrust her.

What gives value to precious gems?
They're exquisite upon her ears.
They lower cleavage and raise hems,
Cutting courtship by many years.

What gives value to crafted gold?
Worn adornment, dazzling delight—
It does not rust when she gets old.
And she'll likely stay overnight.

Kells

The Book of Kells at Trinity
Gives old insights to divinity.
The Long Room encases
Volume of volumes in places
Cased up in cases to infinity.[11]

A Limerick Limerick

A Limerick man named Barney
At a Requiem Mass in Killarney
Sang out of tune so sick
That back in Limerick
They insisted he was from Blarney

Query in a Quarry
The Quarrel of Quincy and Quentin

Quincy and Quentin
Were quarrelsome.
They had no money
And could not borrow some.

A quibble, a riddle,
A quickening grip.
Shaken and startled,
A quizzical quip.

A quest for an answer,
Questions come queasy.
A quiet suggestion,
Quivering and uneasy.

Two men in a quarry—
A quintessential quarrel.
Their quotient of quaintness
Brothers bent over a barrel.

They cornered the quota—
A quantity quartered.
The quintessential question…
How much was ordered?

A happenstance, a glance
Quite the quandary.
A quilt of guilt
Queued to the boundary.

A quake hit the quarry
Their cause for dissentin'
Them and the granite broken,
Quincy cracked Quentin.

The Fall of Spring Training

A reasonably intelligent person
Would shudder to discover
The depths Mortie Mixon would sink
As an avowed baseball lover.

He defrauded them at spring training
Without a reservation or a ticket.
It was a habit he couldn't shake,
Couldn't afford—and couldn't kick it.

He sold programs for the Os at Sarasota,
And scouted the Mets at St. Lucie Port.
He found a ladder at a Tampa outfield fence,
To see the Yankees play as a last resort.

In Lakeland he ushered for the Tigers,
And at Dunedin he sold popcorn for the Jays.
He swept the Braves clubhouse at Lake Buena Vista.
At Port Charlotte, he raked infield for the Rays.

He foraged his way to Phoenix that spring,
As a photographer for the Milwaukee Brewers.
He stayed well distanced from the security there—
Avoiding arrest by MLB fraud pursuers.

But it did come to a "head" in Mesa one night,
When he snuck in as batboy for the Cubs.
A line-drive foul took Mortie Mixon down.
It was a fitting end, courtesy of all MLB clubs.

Near the Outlet of an Inlet

There was a starlet from a hamlet
Wearing bracelets and an anklet
Rivulets flowing to ringlets
Gray-streaked hair in ripplets.

She was dropped from the play
Stricken from the ballet
Offered no role, no more cabaret
The silver screen went away

She threw her billet into the toilet
Cried a tide from her eyelets
The driplets had turned into droplets
She made goblets full of soblets

She took her tablet and her booklet
And created new persona leaflet
Adorned in vivid rose and violets
She aroused the industry eaglets

She now has two valets and three chalets
Wine and petit filets over a blaze
Her singular form became a couplet
Once one down, now a one uplet.

Averse Again Now and Then

Grizzly bear, 2006

Yeti Still Has Nightmares

Little Malcolm asked his Poppa T
For a different bedtime story.
He wanted to face his fears
Through a frightful allegory.
He wouldn't mind a chance meeting
Of a hungry werewolf along the way,
So Poppa T began describing
The looming doom that monsters portray.

They booked a magic fantasy
To Transylvania via Edinburgh,
Where Poppa T figured he might as well
Make the monster list tight and thorough.
The giant Loch Ness serpent was trolling
The cold lake near the highlands.
Malcolm fretted the sighting,
And begged to leave the British Islands.

They went out of their way to see
The happy mermaids and dancing elves—
Then Malcolm suggested it would be nice
To slay a dragon for themselves.
Poppa T knew where the leviathans
And the fire-breathers were hiding.
So he flew his mind to China
As Malcolm's fears began subsiding.

Averse Again Now and Then

They saw an abominable snowman,
A unicorn, and Bigfoot on another trail.
It was a trip never to be forgotten
With zombies and vampires to impale.
He and Poppa T had defeated
Every ghoulish fear posed by Malcolm.
The little tyke had slayed the world,
Though barely out of diapers and talcum.

There's No *O* in Edinburgh

We should celebrate like Rabbie Burns,
And fight to maintain history's treasure.
By raising our glass for the Scotsman
And his heightened appetite for pleasure.

He tosses caber poles end over end;
Blood pudding keeps his hunting dogs frisky
He swears he sees a monster at Loch Ness
Before drinking the *e* out of his whiskey.

He bagpipes his happiness and sorrow away
He's up for eating the haggis, tatties, and neeps
And opening the castle to strangers at night
Because his red-headed wife never sleeps.

He's proud of the Roman aqueduct
And wishes Hadrian's Wall was higher
And the pub tunes roll from his Celtic soul:
"Auld Lang Syne" and "Mull of Kintyre"

He wears his clan's tartan skirt to events
Like the Hogmanay where girls are hottish
He brazenly golfs in the most hellish weather—
It's par for the course in the life of the Scottish.[12]

LY¢PL8s

Ambrose traveled all fifty states
Looking for vanity LY¢PL8s.
The tags had variations of vanity
From ego boasts to hidden profanity.

There was IMATEXN in Dallas
To H82WORK in Corvallis.
There was a DMBG1RL in Ohio
And a GETNKED down on the Bayou.

Expressive support like IM4ART
To enticements like URATART.
Studying traffic in downtown Frisco
Ambrose discovered a 77DISCO.

The keys to life were clearly stated—
BHAPEE and JUSBGUD were plated.
An OK road brought an OUGIRL view,
And a surly but ominous 2L8 4U2.

Identities were discovered down south
Like SNOWHTE, GATSBY, and BGMOUTH.
Arizona was home to CHWBCA and IAMYODA;
CRUZ1N and HEJFUND found in Minnesota.

The exotic automobiles were heralded astutely
Like COP B8, 1SIC BMR, and YELOVET done cutely.
Instructive hints like TIKLME and Y GO SLO
Were seen in Mississippi and Idaho.

Ambrose on the NJ turnpike saw IH8PEAS
And GOOGLME noted with D8MEPLZ.
Warnings in Kansas like STA AWAY
Trumped the BAD IDEA near Mobile Bay.

He followed SY0 NARA to the Upper P,
And 2PRFKT all the way across Tennessee.
The hardest plate to decode he found
Was 370H55V until read upside down.

Must Stash

It was the first treasure that Cornelius ever had—
Large money stacks from his dad's dad's dad.
He thought like a criminal who might break in—
Foregoing the first choice of using his coffee tin.

The obviousness of stuffing it in the mattress
Would precariously present a dubious practice.
He could tape an envelope to the bottom of a shelf.
But it would be found easily by any robber-elf.

Perhaps he could place it in a cookie jar—
Or in a Tupperware container, though bizarre.
He could cut out pages in his family Bible.
Destroying God's Word might incur God's libel.

He could sink it in a sandwich bag into the aquarium,
But the chance of getting it wet was unneccesarium.
A loose board could be the perfect place in the floor,
But his home was carpeted except for the cellar door.

"That's it!" Cornelius exclaimed with zestful glee,
"I'll stick this into the wine cellar, next to the Chablis."
But what poor Cornelius never contemplated—
His Confederate money collection was over-inflated.

Chapter Three

Making Sense of Where and Whence

View of sailboat on the Thunersee, Switzerland, 2005

Know Your Phobia

Upon the Great Depression,
The words of Franklin Delano Roosevelt,
Described the ultimate phobia of all phobias,
The fear of fear itself.

People have fear for good reason,
Because fear keeps us sensible.
If we didn't have fear of heights,
We might do something reprehensible.

Among our greatest of fears is pteromerhanophobia,
Known as fear of flying.
For some of us, it even exceeds thanatophobia,
The somber fear of dying.

Glossophobia tops the list of all phobias
From Buffalo to Peking.
It's accepted as the highest anxiety known—
Fear of public speaking.

If someone has a combination of fears
It's a difficult mental condition.
It can't be treated over the telephone,
(Latrophobia is the fear of physicians).

Cryophobia, one might guess is the fear of crying;
But it's not that at first glance.
It's a fear of being frozen,
Cryophobics do not ski for the fear of an avalanche.

Perhaps the most unique fear
That fellow phobians detest the most
Is phobophobia, or the fear of fear—
Like a night watchman who fears a ghost.

Nurse Eerie Verse

If you imagine Nightingale
In her flowing *nightingown*,
It should warrant Florence
To pull her nightshades down.

Magic-Carpet Stride

We know that mustachioed Alp Arslan[13]
Lived his life a disturbed Seljuk sultan.
He won fame at the Battle of Manzikert,
And killed those captured who wouldn't convert.

Tied behind his neck like a taut bullwhip
Were the long whiskers of his upper lip.
Because of the battle plans Alp Arslan chose,
The Byzantines fell as Persians rose.

A captured captain with nothing to lose
Rushed Arslan's cot as he began to snooze.
The casual Alp paused to load his bow,
But tripped on the rug, and received the blow.

Alp Arslan lingered two days hence,
Then died of an ironic happenstance.
The captain escaped dodging conversion.
The rug Alp Arslan tripped on was Persian.

Whacko Zack
With Antisesquipedalian Sentimentalities

Zack was a thin bald man who had no direction.
He felt that he was under the devil's control.
He wandered into caves and high over mountains—
Walking everywhere to find the good in his soul.

He was stunned by the stark realities of truth.
He found the calmness of its meaning, though bitter.
He long desired to become a journalist.
Instead, he hid among the rocks as a quitter.

Wounded by life, Zack did something unexpected.
He built a large fire of sparse twigs on a mound.
He left quickly as the flames reached the dried brush.
Somehow he knew that fire's meaning was profound.

Zack's abilities were wasted by inaction.
His life depended upon the devil's shortcuts.
But the weight of his past failures billowed away
Like the smoke dancing in the flames as Zack went nuts.[14]

An Esoteric Sesquipedalian Epitaph
More a Taradiddle than a Tale

Zachariah was leptosome and pilgarlic.
He suffered from cacodemonomania.
He was a spelunker and a montivagant—
Perambulating ubiquitous noegenesis.
His flummoxed moment transpired
With the dichotomy of equanimity,
And flouting undeniable acrimony.
Though scripturient, he remained saxicolous.
As he was a deleterious defeatist,
The oddly anomalistic Zachariah
Erected a parsimonious conflagration.
Brazenly, hastily he absquatulated.
His excogitation revealed absurdity.
The man became an unencumbered panurgic.
The smolder pattern seemed to exorcise demons.
Zachariah transmuted into widdershins.[15]

Spelchekked

It is imminently pawsable
To circumvent the spell Czech feature of yore calm pewter.
Eye now no how to purr form this fee ask Co.
Ewe just have to right words buy they're sounds.
Two a purr son list ten inn,
Their is know odd able differ rinse.
Butt too a copy Ed deter,
This A Bomb in nation is awe fully pro found.

Hiram on High

Hiram passed away last Thursday
Facing an unknown spiritual destiny.
He was grieved by his three children
And his loving wife Penelope.
His final destination was waylaid
By an unassuming sense, it seems—
Hiram was deeply introverted
And lived by paranoiac extremes.

His soul was directed toward
A place he found quite confusing.
At first glance, it would not have been
A place of his personal choosing.
He saw the banker there who refused
To approve a needed business loan,
And the schoolmate's parent whom he crossed
When he served as a chaperone.

Sitting in the corner was the teacher
Who flunked him in sixth-grade math.
The minister Foley was also there—
Hiram assumed he was a psychopath!
Near them—a lawyer who was disbarred—
Hiram had come to admire him;
And across the room—Aunt Judy—
Who suggested naming him Hiram.

There was the little league umpire that
Called him out on a dubious pitch,

Averse Again Now and Then

And the fellow from the corner shop
Who fixed his grill-regulator switch.
It was that failed grill switch
That ended his early retirement plan.
It sparked the line that fired the blast
That shortened Hiram's lifespan.

Hiram was queasy in this odd waiting room
He vaguely exchanged a greeting,
Not knowing if he was in heaven or hell
Based upon the souls who held the seating.
He realized that all those assembled
Had done him an ignoble service—
But those disfavors back in his lifetime
Made his curious spirit more nervous.

Angels that were guides helping Hiram
To enter heaven's first room—
He met each of them along life's path,
Averting horrific eternal doom.
Even the person who botched the switch
That set off his gas grill regulator,
Was there to support and expedite him
As if he was a God-sent collaborator.

When Hiram arrived he did not know
He was guided on earth to the right place.
He thought he had gone to hell and that
There was a short in God's database.

W. Thomas McQueeney

Once he found familiar angels in heaven,
His innate introversion soon subsided.
When he asked their purpose for meeting him there,
They said they were angels of the misguided.

John Dark

The life of Joan of Arc inspires a saintly audience.
She disguised herself as a man when she heard voices.
She bravely defeated the invading English at Orleans,
But her commanding royalty exercised other choices.

Youthful Joanie was detained as if she were a witch.
They feared her popularity had gotten out of control.
She scored a triumph for women and made her niche—
Even the stuffy bourgeoisie had to admit she was on a roll.

A horrible end was in store for this keeper of peace.
They sentenced her to death with all royal decrees in.
She was burned at the stake wearing her fleur-de-lis
After being charged with treason in the Age of Unreason.

Centuries later, when visiting the French countryside,
One would rarely hear her name as Joan of Arc.
The French pronounce this saint as if to bluntly chide
Her disguise as a man, calling her "John Dark."[16]

Cabo San Lucas sunrise, 2006

The Manner of the Manor

Hector was always confusing the autobahn
With the man who catalogued the species of birds.
He mistakenly thought of John James Audubon—
As he heard two audibly identical words.

Hector knew that there were many word precedents.
He listed all the homophones one could expect.
He went to professors and college presidents
Citing too much sounding confusion to neglect.

In a series, they become a serial—
But in milk they become a cereal.
Homophones cause puzzling sighs
From puzzled people of every size.

Hector wrote a book of sounds, a first edition;
And lobbied its use in schools at the capitol.
But when he needed to make a new addition,
The book publisher required a lot more capital.

Hector's purpose was among the highest intents.
The politicians saw his objective was not hostile.
But raising public money is incredibly intense,
So Hector made his stately home into a hostel.

He opened it for students traveling alone.
And fed them a hearty breakfast ev'ry morning.
But then Hector died while still paying down a loan.
It was repossessed while his wife was still mourning.

In a series, they become a serial—
But in milk they become a cereal.
Homophones cause puzzling sighs
From puzzled people of every size.

Love Of

Of seems to be a word
That creates high historical belonging,
Citing origins **of** someplace
Or **of** some significance in performing.
Belonging **of** some experience
Can mean a life's eroding—
Like the Tower **of** London, the Passage **of** Time,
Each **of** each one foreboding.
One could be the Rock **of** Ages,
The Rose **of** Tralee, or the Son **of** Sam;
Or a Leap **of** Faith friar like Francis **of** Assisi,
Gentle as a lamb.

Eleanor **of** Aquitaine was
The eventual mother **of** two kings.
Ignatius **of** Loyola was a knight **of** Spain,
Among many other things.
Catherine **of** Aragon was the first wife
Of England's Henry the Eighth.
Joan **of** Arc was a martyr known
For bravado in the keeping **of** her faith.
The Duke **of** Wellington won his fame
At the Battle **of** Waterloo.
Helen **of** Troy was **of** radiant beauty,
By Homer's epic review.

Have you ever heard **of** other *ofs*
Like Vincent **of** Beauvais?

He was the priest who wrote our history down
In encyclopedic array.
How about Herbert **of** Cherbury,
Who is considered the father **of** deism?
Or Teresa **of** Ávila, one of the first females
To defend Christian theism?
We shall not forget Philip **of** Hesse,
Whose army backed the Reformation,
Or William **of** Sens, whose architectural gifts
Built cathedral installations.

If one is not an "**of**" listed above,
There is no cause **of** despair.
You're **of** your time, passing prime,
And **of** a paradigm somewhere.[17]

The Out-the-Door Commodore

Matthew C. Perry scheduled a way
To find significance in every living day.
He sailed into serendipity it somehow seems
Charting maps full of sailor's dreams.

The "father of the navy's first steamed fleet";
Fathom him as father to twenty little feet.
He commanded ships in three American wars.
And sailed into Tokyo to open trading doors.

He claimed Key West away from the Spanish,
And made the Barbary Pirates all but vanish.
Dutifully to the West Indies he was assigned;
When offered a post by the Russians, but declined.

At the Naval Academy, he established courses,
Before becoming Commodore of US Forces.
He was later honored as plenipotentiary to Japan.
Matt Perry had become a true Renaissance man.

Gallant in his travels, Perry authored a book—
Historians cite Farragut and Halsey but still overlook
The man who died after nearly fifty years at sea…
How he timed fathering ten children is still beyond me.[18]

Chronologies of Other Times

My old
Clock is mistaken.
It must be! I fell asleep at
Ten-oh-three. Awakened by silence,
It says it's nearly one. It seems my energy
For remembering has dissipated. Time has ticked
Away ever so quietly—unless heard at night. Must the
Dimensions of light, space, and time each pulse within
Cadences of accepted metered limits—silent and scary?
My eyes are bleary and forlorn. When my life began
It seemed that ticks and tocks had reversed, unaware
Of their own unraveling. A blessed future emerged.
The sheer anticipation and exuberance of living
Beckoned before me. No clock bore warning.
It seems that time toyed with a delay in
Each day's marking of each hour.
Eternity the higher power,
I watched clocks
Waiting
For
Summer or
Christmas. It was as if
Every clock had paused and
Laughed at my impatience. A day was
A week. In a recurring dream time slowly sped
Each calendar digit away from my innocent youth.
Those memories run together into distant moments
That marked their vague reference to now. The *blink*
Only travels backwards. Sadly, the short in the clock
Retraces nothing special in between. The thought is
Serene and disturbing. It distorts the past into an era.
As this age meets each new sunrise, the time that
Went away is both longer and shorter each day.
A clock is a failure. Lesser seconds make up
Lesser minutes. Age directs as life crawls
Within its shadow. Still, my clock is
Wrong. It will stay that way
Until time consumes
All else…gone.

Chapter Four

Coyotes and Foxes

Laughing Rodrigo

Laughing Rodrigo remembered when he was taking his bath
That the door was unlocked and Iris was on the warpath.
He could not for his life recall for which reason she was—
Vehement and violent screaming is just what she did and does.

He remembered to buy her gifts on each of the holidays,
And just assumed that she was just going through a phase.
But she continued to scold him mercilessly nonetheless,
Calling it menopause, her permit for her unpleasantness.

Rodrigo felt he couldn't take her loud tirades any longer.
His baths were a necessary hygienic for his job, a fishmonger.
As the decibel level got closer to where he was soaking,
He went under the water and started coughing and choking.

Iris came running to the tub to see if Rodrigo was drowning,
But immediately went crazy when she saw he was clowning.
Iris was fired up angry, until Rodrigo flung water and doused her.
The extension cord never shorted out when Iris threw in the toaster.

Shem Creek, Mt. Pleasant, SC, at sunset, 2012

Ineffable Ed

They said that Ed was ineffable.[19]
His standing was nebulously hued.
What he was sipping was unclear—
Our view of the setting was skewed.

The candle diffused his corner table.
The ambient light distorted him.
Perhaps Ed had become invisible then
By the shadows that had escorted him.

Indistinctly, he rose from his seat,
Undefined by a fortune acquired.
He lived his vague life deceptively.
One night, indubitably, Ed expired.

Nobody could figure where his money went,
The probate judge found no stash.
His fortune was a mystery in a riddle spent—
Ed was ineffable enough to not need cash.

We never witnessed Ed to laugh aloud—
Never knew him to confide or jest.
To say that Ed was an ineffable soul—
Who knows? Only God may have guessed.

Do Not Go Mental, Brother!
Here's to You, Dylan Thomas!

Do not grow mental from your hindsight,
Old age makes you learn to look the other way;
Crazy, crazy to be crying in the night.

Though wise men sense the frantic and fright—
Hoping their dreams will flicker, and fade away,
Do not grow mental from your hindsight!

Good men mask their eyes, knowing how slight
Their failed deeds may have passed, don't they?
Crazy, crazy to be crying in the night.

Mild men who sought and hailed the moon's delight
Learned, too late, and grieved time's decay.
Do not grow mental from your hindsight!

Brave men, near death, shield the blinding light,
Their eyes on fire like a meteor's display—
Crazy, crazy to be crying in the night.

Do you, my brother, find sadness in spite—
Cursed or blessed by the nightmares that stay?
Do not grow mental from your hindsight!
Crazy, crazy to be crying in the night.[20]

DD Sick

David Devane attended early school
With dubious kinks in his gene pool.
He was rotund with a gaunt-like face,
And left his boogers everyplace.
His sinuses were a total mess.
The limp was caused by anyone's guess.
His inhaler was always in his pocket,
And he wore a patch on one eye socket.
After years of missing classes while sick,
He graduated with a walking stick.
We never saw "DD" as years flew by,
And never wondered exactly why.
He was off the radar until one day,
He qualified to withdraw his 401k.
The man had miserly saved every penny.
Not lavishing friends—he didn't have many.
He cheated on taxes and stole from charities.
Retiring before they discovered disparities.
He was free to do whatever he would
Limited by what he couldn't and could.
David Devane was incredibly wealthy,
Surviving for years being most unhealthy.
His heart disease had gotten worse,
So he hired a permanent personal nurse.
His diabetes required daily insulin,
Chased down by a handful of Ritalin.
Crohn's disease made his travel cautious—
Multiple medications made him nauseous.
We all yearned for cures, as we got old,

To find new remedies for the common cold.
David Devane must have done this, too.
And maybe he found a cure for the flu.
No one could imagine his daily strife.
He was lousy liver of a terrible life.
I read that David Devane died one day.
His obituary that morning had much to say.
He was sick of life and sick of us, too.
DD Sick overdosed on the cure for the flu.

Embrace Your Glacier

Embrace your
Glacier.
Where ice
Has dwelt
For an eon,
And polar bears
And penguins
Pee on.
Eventually,
Conventionally
To melt
To water
For the otter
When it gets hotter.

Embrace your
Glacier.
Rivers depend
On where
They end.
A spring drip
Makes a
Very long trip
Down the ravine
In a forward lean
At a snail-like clip.

Embrace your
Glacier
They recede
For blocks
And reveal
New rocks
Moving slow
With weighty snow
Grinding grist
Turn and twist
A creepy show
From centuries ago.

Embrace your
Glacier.
At every crevice.
Toast with Chivas.
And be glad
Your comrade
Didn't fall
Down endless walls
Of a crevasse.
He'd bust his arse.
A farce—
Forever frozen
Head to toes in

A chiseled face
Displaced
With no trace
Glaciers
Are nature's sensatiers.
They're a cold space
To decompose in.

His First Name Was Lloyd

Mr. Llewellyn was confounded
About the way his name resounded.
After much muttering
And constant stuttering
Mr. Lou Ellen was founded.

Amen Corner at Augusta National Golf Course, 2011

Declan Twomey

Declan Twomey loved potatoes
But only three times a day.
He tried to switch to cauliflower—
Though his taste was for potato soufflé.

For breakfast, he liked tater tots,
For lunch he ate cheese fries.
For dinner, he craved his potato baked
With butter, sour cream, and chives.

He could always find a bag of chips
Or hash browns scattered as treats.
No place on the planet for pomegranate—
In Paris, he wolfed down pomme frites.

No menu could deny his starchy diet
Declan was a russet connoisseur.
He ordered bangers and mash by the Thames
Until he couldn't eat spuds anymore.

He lost forty pounds in just two months—
When the wardrobe of Declan Twomey
Cloaked his former rotund frumpy figure—
His suits were too large and roomy.

He ate carrots and cornflakes for a solid year.
His friends marveled at how thin he'd gotten.
But alas, he was honored at a dinner party
And couldn't pass up the casserole au gratin.

He stuffed himself with large croquettes
And ate fried wedges from his potato-filled dish.
He gained a hundred pounds in a hundred days
Without even sampling the potato knish.

He trudged around at four hundred pounds
Until he could no longer stand the hecklin'.
The *Pomme de Terre* assuaged his fear—
The spud on the street was unshakably indiscreet—
The falling thud was unmistakably Declan.

Frogs and Turtles

Turtles are serendipitous.
They move about unconcerned.
Once they sense any of us,
Their journey is adjourned.

Frogs belong in asylums.
They play out in the rain.
We rarely hear them in daytime.
At night they croak insane.

It seems their lives are similar—
Amphibians moving slow.
We allow them to freely pass
To beach, or bay, or archipelago.

That's because they're crazy, you know.

The Curious Case of Yimmy Jager
Frustrations Wound Like a JoJo

Golf is a game that requires intensity
With pro tips recalled in all their immensity.
It's difficult to enjoy unless played well—
Any distraction at all, and your game goes to hell.

A partner's a plus when he's on his game—
Quiet, sedate, and in a competitive frame.
But, oh, how a score can easily balloon,
Playing with a cad, a chump, or a bumbling buffoon!

I was next at the tee paired with Yimmy Jager—
Greg Norman Collection shirt, slacks by Haggar.
Consistently he unleashed a most horrendous hook,
Calling it a "yerk" with each swing he took.

He'd miss short putts because they made him nervous
Saying he had the "jips," the pronunciation curious.
He'd "jank" out his five-iron for a mighty swat,
Then "jell" at the ball as he whiffed his shot.

He'd address each attempt with a quirky "yiggle."
Then look up as I grimaced; it made him giggle.
He'd punch another worm-burner down the course,
Amassing many strokes with errors unforced.

My inquiry was made of his misuse of the *Y*.
He noted that it's the curse by which all Jagers comply.
There were Yeagers and Jaegers and Jaggers pronounced
Exactly the same sound, by all accounts.

Averse Again Now and Then

He continued to whack away at his own behest.
Reporting scores to write down which appeared in "yest."
I happened to be golfing with Yimmy Jager the day
That his mind went berserk on words starting with *J*.

Through more than a hundred strokes I'd persevered
As Yimmy kept muttering his pronunciations weird.
I finally broke by the riverside on his next errant shot.
When he spotted a Yetski, and called it a "Jacht."

I ranted uncontrollably and cursed like a sailor—
And slung my driver, then snapped my railer.
I charged toward Yimmy to give him a choking.
But resorted to laughter when he said, "I'm yoking."

Left unto Thyself

What would I do without you?
I'd miss the many quirks about you.
I'd invite a crowd,
Turn the music loud,
And with heavy drink,
I'd sit and think,
In a dizzying hue
Of the things I'd do
Without you.

I'd raise cats—Siamese—
And set the temp to seventy degrees
I'd wear browns with blues
With whatever shoes
I'd have near.
I wouldn't care.
There'd be plenty of new things
I'd happily plan to do
Without you.

I'd make a pass
At a younger lass
Who'd no doubt
Turn me out.
I'd be made a sap,
But I'd just tip my cap—
And go on to
Yet another lass to woo.
She might try to woo me too
Without you.

Averse Again Now and Then

My public reign
Without "ball and chain"
Would flourish yet—
As I'd pirouette,
I'd place my bet
With newfound spontaneity.
Perhaps, I'd be like deity
Until my life is through,
Doing all I wanted to do
Without you.

My darkened days
Could have lighted ways
With no one near
No cold stare
No more nagging to bear
Or brazen innuendo—
No arguing crescendo!
You'd wonder if I'm blue
Or where I'd be headed to
Without you.

You'd load ketchup on your steak—
Have one less bed to make—
No me there to forsake.
There'd be no project list,
No fate left for you to twist.
Surely, I wouldn't be missed.
You'd burn the chair that I liked best—

Throw my things into a box addressed
To someone you thought you knew.
But you didn't really know.
We'd say we gave it a go.
Then we'd start anew.
You'd be free
To do anything you see
Worthy to do—
Without me,
And me without you

Obits are the Pits

No more funerals are required of me.
I went to two last week,
And the week before I went to three.

I'm sixty-five and now retired
The old friends and family I have gained
Have lived, laughed, loved, and expired.

I've noticed all of the lovely flowers
I dressed in a suit for each visitation—
Standing in line for endless hours.

What can one do that might have mattered?
A death is a final status irreversible—
Expect the family to be emotionally shattered.

People falsely admire the ashen look—
A last coffin view of the sadly deceased.
Don't forget to sign the guest book.

The formal services is held the next day.
The celebrant will assume heaven's destination,
I knew some who were given much leeway.

The burial is often held in private,
But sometimes friends assemble in a tent.
Attendance depends on the weather to drive it.

W. Thomas McQueeney

After-receptions are not uncommon events.
A cheese cracker or a stiff drink is fine.
At the last one I discovered my commonsense.

If ten funerals for forty years should combine,
Then four hundred funerals would produce
Not one person I honored who could attend mine.

Chapter Five

More Stars, Same Stripes

The following fifty presentations are tributes to the fifty states of the United States of America in reverse order of each states' admittance to the Union.

View of Maui sunset, 2009

Breezes in the Treezes

The only non-American Americans live
On the archipelago of Hawaii.
It's painful for the natives to forgive
How we absconded Kahoolawe.

There's nothing cool on Kahoolawe.
In fact, the islands thrive upon lava.
Waterfalls fall from Oahu to Kauai,
And the Kona bean is king of the java.

There's a banyan tree in Port Lahaina,[21]
Not far from the murder of Captain Cook.
Its roots grow through almost to China—
Whale watchers climb it to take a look.

By dawn the sun rises above Aloha clouds
Of Mount Haleakala, two miles high.
The tempestuous Mona Kea enshrouds
Soothing temperatures on down to Molokai.

The fiftieth state and its Diamond Head
Is a surfer's paradise for its pipelines.
Serene pineapple groves are widespread.
Dancing wahinis bring out the sunshine.

Oh, the tropical flowers that adorn Hawaii!
The seabirds whisk by the winds of trade.
If I have but one wish before I die-e,
It's to arrive there again and be properly lei'd.

Aleut Aloof

"Native Americans" came to Alaska
When the icy Bering was straight.[22]
The Asian wanderers headed south,
But the adventurous moved upstate.

Those who hunted the polar bears,
And Kodiaks, and nesting salmon—
Found the Yukon and the North Slope,
And lakes that couldn't be swam in.

If warmth you want in an igloo
The firewood—you must bring it.
You can rub noses with their kinfolk,
Whether a Malamute or a Tlingit.

If a native tribesman wants a suntan,
The village would find it apropos
To send him to the Inside Passage—
It's the Alaskan Riviera to the Eskimo.

Enjoy the expanse of the forty-ninth state
And meet the native peoples there.
Salute an Aleut; buy an Eskimo suit,
Or just get Inuit on a dare.

Averse Again Now and Then

Mendenhall Glacier view, 2006

Arizonian

Route 66 curves through Winslow
In a desert past endless sand.
The tempo has always been slow
From Tempe to the Canyon Grand.

The heavens of ancient ages—
Where meteors fell from the sky.
A giant crater upstages
Attractive Winslow sites nearby.

The Peublo and the Navajo
Are native Arizonians.
Their languages remain although
They thrive as living Smithsonians.

Phoenix is a metropolis
To include Mesa and Scottsdale.
It's a giant megalopolis
Where all traffic slows to a snail.

A favorite place to visit—
Monument Valley Monoliths.
You're sure to ask, "What is it?"
Sedate in a state full of myths.

Thirty-five species of scorpions
Traverse the tumbleweed desert.
Don't pet the big fuzzy ones—
They consider humans pay dirt.

New Mexicode

The land enchants
With Yucca plants
Adobe abode
Sunsets explode
Snake-dance tunes
Hot-air balloons
Beef jerky
Albuquerque
Water shortage
No port or portage
Gadsden Purchase
Border-crossing searches
Carlsbad Caverns
Wind-worn taverns
Flying objects unidentified
Roswell sightings coincide
Real Apache chief
Really Georgia O'Keeffe
Trail to Santa Fe
Native macrame
Heightened sense of senses
Truth or Consequences
Roadrunners galore
Home of Demi Moore
Chili jars stacked high
Fully landscaped cacti
Los Alamos facility
Oil and gas stability
No place for a yachter

High demand for water
Bisected by Interstate 10
Turn and return again!

Home of Roger Miller

Okla and *Humma* are Choctaw words
Meaning "people shaded red."[23]
Oklahoma has reservations full of natives
Who didn't reserve ahead.
There are oaken barrels full of Okies
That made it to the national stage—
A veritable virtuoso of performers
From the current and prior age.

Who doesn't like Reba McEntire?
Or Carrie Underwood, for that matter?
Or Brad Pitt, James Garner, Ron Howard?
All are stars from the dustbowl platter.
A baseball commercial from Commerce hailed—
Known as the great Mantle, Mick.
Garth Brooks and Toby Keith strum country tunes
Making Sooners much sooner homesick.

A thousand people live in Beckham County,
Mostly huddled in tiny Erick, OK.
It's midway from the east coast to the west
And not much out of anybody's way.
You should park near the corner
Of Sheb Wooley Avenue and old Route 66.
You'd enjoy seeing the museum there
A converted drugstore made of red bricks.

There ain't no other place like it;
A one-of-a-kind songwriter's thriller.

W. Thomas McQueeney

It's the oddly located, understated, and underrated—
The outdated museum of Roger Miller.
There are fewer fans there than he deserved,
And it has fewer accolades than he was awarded.
As a writer he wrote the oddest tunes
Of all the oddest tunes ever recorded.

"My Uncle Used to Love Me but She Died"
"Dang Me," and "One Dyin and a Buryin"
Became wonderfully crafted tunes to hum
This museum is as good as any aquarium.

Cheers to the place where the state drink is milk,
And Miller emerged with robust distinction.
He was asked what Erick, Oklahoma, was near,[24]
And he coyly answered, "Extinction."[25]
The museum has many scripts, notes, and artifacts
Of the unsung singer to sing his praises
Say what you want about Roger Miller,
But the man could really turn a few phrases.

Sense for Census

The most intriguing state
And most beguiling history
Is bundled together by fate
In the Utah mating mystery.

It's like nothing you ever saw in
Any place and anywhere
Seeing a polygamist Utahan
Fill out lines on a questionnaire.

If he's a full-fledged member—
A fundamentalist Mormon,
A quick-family assembler
He's not used to conformin'.

He might fill out twenty tykes
And add six subservient wives.
Their Utah census number hikes
As each newborn Utahan arrives.

He must be listening closely
When he adjusts to "Mountain Time."
If his mates approach him cozily,
And it's not a mounting he can climb.

In fact, the Mormons are known
For the vices they commonly forsake.
Each husband's reason to postpone
Is by common excuse—a headache!

Evening view from Patriot's Point, 2009

Suffering Suffrage

Cowboys have the umbrage
In ever-lowered numbrage
To ride the fencing coverage
To protect the cattle overage.

A blanket, a kettle, no luggage—
A pint of rye with his porridge.
A night for the rite of passage.
Fearing no animal nor any savage.

When home he finds advantage
To embrace the bonds of marriage,
His wife requires a carriage—
Without a whimpering disparage.

They're off to vote their votage,
Agreeing politics is making sausage.
Wyoming's known for the rough age
When it championed women's suffrage.

A cowboy will assume the steerage.
The reins in his hands are his peerage.
Tis time to show his stern courage,
To vote as she directs into his dotage.

Hi-Dee-Ho

All of New England could fit into Idaho,
It's the home of the poet Ezra Pound.
Harmon Killebrew grew up in Payette—
Few celebrities are in Idaho found.

They grow potatoes near Pocatello.
You can find them up in Coeur d'Alene.
They even grow them outside of Boise—
And on most of the farms in between.

Idaho farmers are the hardiest of folks
They are celebrated for their toil.
When they scoop into dirt with their burly hands
Potatoes emerge from their Idaho soil.

It's potatoes, not gems in the Gem State,
That can bring the economy to its knees.
Let's face it—spuds are a national staple—
And perfect potatoes don't grow on trees.

Anorexics on Diets

There are no echoes coming from Puget Sound.
And Bellingham has no bell or ham.
The Tacoma coffee shops are not Seattle-renowned
With WiFi, odd fragrances, and live webcam.

The earth is essential to the people of Seattle.
They stage rallies, protests, sit-ins, and riots.
Yet there is one intolerable flaw there that'll
Rub them forever wrong; it's anorexics on diets.

They have sushi to expand any tushy,
Fresh fish on every platter and ev'ry dish.
You want tofu? Seattleites will cook, you see—
Plates of hummus, pâté, tilapia, and knish.

In the Great Northwest, where dining is hectic—
The restaurants sample every Pacific Rimmer—
Rendering culinary sensation to foods eclectic
For foodies, connoisseurs, and each skeptic skimmer.

One would guess that the Dungeness, a crustacean,
Would be from a dungeon or lair or den
It's the tastiest crab of all crabs of all creation.
Or try free-range chicken or deranged hen.

Upon closer inspection with culinary perfection
We should take the time to further examine…
Anorexics would never diet in this state northwestern,
They'd go restaurant to restaurant eating salmon.

To Helena Hand Basket

The nation's fourth largest state is the last best place
To find serenity and purposely meander.
The Little Bighorn—a river that's named for sheep—
Allows crossings by a short leap—a bridgeless wonder.

The parks have views that postcards cannot fathom—
There's no sky higher than The Big Sky.
Cowboys ride fences on ranches, their sense is
Miles City dwellers don't let Missoulians drop by.

The Rockies divide Montana on two sides,
Yet there's plenty of grassland for cattle and bison.
Fly fishing streams and other outdoor extremes—
It's no state for a psychiatrist to give advice in.

Rodeo heroes have fractured hundreds of bones
Riding broncos, roping calves and steers.
It's a man's man who can tame rugged Montana,
Facing coyotes, wolves, mountain lions, and bears.

Glacier Park is likely the craggiest place of all,
Where the forests hide those who want to get lost.
In Red Lodge and Bozeman, they divert the tourists—
While nightly in Billings, the Hooligans get sauced.

With colorful places like Hungry Horse Dam,
Bear Dance, Anaconda, Nimrod, and Two Dot,
This great western state has room for all comers
Like Ted Turner—yes—but Jane Fonda—not!

Averse Again Now and Then

If the devil finds rascals in quiet little Helena,
The question—should one hesitantly ask it—
Where are you taking me with that pitchfork, Dude—
And why are we headed to Helena hand-basket?

Arch at confluence of the Pacific and Sea of Cortez, Cabo San Lucas, 2006

Chapter Six

West by Midwest Zest

The Preacher in Pierre, SD

A clever pastor at a parish in Pierre
Got a visit from an agent of the IRS.
He asked if his flock showed a Roy Lehrer,
The inquisitive pastor replied, "Well, yes."

The agent asked if he kept donation records.
He asked if in his ledger he'd check
If Roy Lehrer made a sizeable donation
Meant to fund their All Saints Choir Deck.

The pastor asked how much the donor submitted
So that he could spot the entered amount until—
The IRS agent surprised him saying $10,000 was sent.
The pastor replied, "Whether I find it or not, he will!"

Big Fur Coat

If Fargo to North Dakota,
I'd take a big fur coat.
Minot ever go outside—
I'd have it there to tote.

If Fargo to North Dakota,
I'd plan a trip to Bismarck.
Minot go in wintertime—
Spring's when I'd embark.

If Fargo to North Dakota,
I'd hunt Canadian geese.
Minot have any success—
At least, I'd shoot my piece.

If Fargo to North Dakota,
I'd stand by the painted cow.[26]
Minot meet anybody there—
I'd find some fun somehow.

If Fargo to North Dakota,
I'm sure I would get married.
Minot find the girl I want—
Everything's cash and carried.

If Fargo to North Dakota,
I'd ask if I could work there.
Minot find an indoor job—
But I'd have a big fur coat to wear.

Colorado

Echoes echo,
Colorado.
Western Mountains
Eastern Plains
Continental Divide
Telluride
Giant sand dunes
Denver Tunes
Hiking
Biking
Living healthy
Very wealthy
Colorado Springs
Air Force wings
Wild horses
Natural resources
Lodge honeys
Snow bunnies
Oregon Trail
Vail
Wooded thickets
Lift tickets
Fresh air
Sky is clear
Gasp in
Aspen
Surprises galore
Broadmoor
American eagle
Dope is legal.

Omaha "Steaks" Claim for Baseball

The outline of Nebraska is mindful
Of a railroad train's diesel engine—
Set to the east and pulling
A load of Wyoming by extension.
Plains give way to fertile valleys;
Shade trees gather the cows.
They started Arbor Day in Nebraska,
Serenading cottonwoods then and now.

It's absurd that Omaha pins its identity
To a college baseball's major event.
Champions were crowned on a field
That heralds the college they each represent.
Rosenblatt Stadium was torn down
To expand the Henry Doorly Zoo.
A new stadium was built nearby
The Creighton Bluejays play there too.

Grain is king in the corny state.
There's a maizy maze of stalks.
They take conservatism very seriously
They're fond of pheasants, but big on hawks.
Gasoline contains the smell of ethanol;
A mix that fuels tractors near Lincoln.
When one passes through Colon, Nebraska—
The irony is that the town ain't stinkin'.

Averse Again Now and Then

Hibernian Back Bar, Charleston, SC, 2007

Economic Data from Nevada

"Dere's gold in them dere hills."
Well, there was…and silver, too.
But it wasn't the hills that made
Nevada into its modern identity.
It was another public commodity
That brought in more money than
All its gold and silver combined.
Though both are still mined,
The entrepreneurs found
Profit above ground,
Something easy
To market and
Believe in.
Selling
Sin
!

Leslie Down from the Holler

Leslie came on down from the holler to the hardware store.
    He said he'd been to places that raised many a brow.
    First he spouted that he'd just got back from Ottawa—
And just before that trip, he'd gone back and forth to Glasgow.

Leslie had been in those mountains for too many years,
    And most people never paid him much attention.
    A few years ago he bragged that he had been to Venus—
It was via a Sun trip, then to Pluto in another dimension.

    He persisted by describing places far away like London.
    He stopped by on that same jaunt to see Vienna and Berlin.
He rattled off Rangoon, Burma, and Shanghai as worth seeing.
It was likely that Leslie had been drinking spoiled bathtub gin.

He was never challenged by the locals who knew of his delusions.
    He cited Cuba, Ireland, Porto Rico, and Palestine
        for their disorders.
They winked. Leslie had never left the mountains of West Virginia,
And each of the places Leslie tallied were indeed within its borders!

Oh Kansas, My Kansas!

Kansas had a fiery baptism.
In fact, they called it bloody.
Their fortunes did not elevate
The state's a calamity study.
History notes a windstorm came,
And took away the Kansas soil.
Kansas farmers were devastated,
By their loss of earnest toil.

Bankers marked farmers' checks
For a "funds insufficient" return—
Which puzzled the Kansas farmers—
They had deposited all they earned.
Receipts proved their balances true,
The cashiers smiled and said, "Thanks."
It wasn't the farm accounts that were low,
But rather the bankrupt banks!

Wealthy financial elites who employed
So many blue-collar Kansans
Fell with the markets while trading stocks
Once meant to earn bonanzans.
But as their fortunes dwindled down,
And no more financial windfalls came—
They couldn't pay the boarding schools,
So had to learn their children's names.

Averse Again Now and Then

With no food, no industry, no money,
No crops, and no topsoil layer to till,
Kansas became a state of desolation,
Awaiting a new destiny to fulfill.
Con men came as preachers
To exorcise demons and dispossess them.
But Kansas farmers exposed their lies,
And in the process repossessed them.

The new Kansas is a model state,
Where hardworking farmers united.
Their penchant for overcoming duress
Warrants investors there excited.
You can poll the mindset of most
Adventuresome Americans now—
By visiting a modern Kansas farm
To learn the old way to milk a new cow.

Spa or Salon in Oregon

Nora Lynda Bea lived near Beaverton.
Her sister, Constance, also lived there.
They decided to open a spa in Salem—
With Connie's boyfriend, Charlie Weir.

They bought tanning beds from Corvallis.
The bank extended their credit line.
They bought oils and soaps from Portland.
They hired a decorator for interior design.

They bought wind chimes and bird sounds,
And an array of incense from the Orient.
They installed waterfalls and mud baths.
Their slippers and robes were luxuriant.

Charlie Weir lent them his savings account
Just before he proposed to Connie Bea.
Nora Lynda drained her 401k
To spur a successful spa guarantee.

Charlie eloped with Connie one night,
But Constance Bea Weir couldn't foresee,
The bank got nervous and called their note,
Thus, neither a borrower Nora Lynda Bea.

Dale Köester

It was just this side
Of Mankato, Minn.
Where Dale Köester left
His ice-fishing mother.
She begged him to stay
And enjoy the walleye,
But he had plans to move
Further souther.

Minnesota has lakes
Where the natives angle.
The addiction to fishing
Overcomes a freeze.
They catch pike and crappie,
Perch and trout,
It's habit, not a hobby—
It's more a disease.

Dale Köester pursued
His southern career
And settled in Georgia
Near Decatur.
His mother fell into
A frozen lake;
Köester scurried home
To liquidate her.

Minneapolis to Mankato,
He hastily hurried—

W. Thomas McQueeney

His old haunt demanded
Tribute for his only ancestor.
No ice for fishing in Georgia—
No walleye or pike—
Yet, lamenting the last day
Mankato saw Momma Köester.

Minnesota has lakes
Where the natives angle.
The addiction to fishing
Overcomes minus five degrees.
They catch pike and crappie,
Perch and trout,
It's habit, not a hobby—
Dale Köester tired of the freeze.

Brendan and Brandon

Brendan was stuck on the five not moving—
　　Brandon on the fifteen rolling in smog.
　They smothered LA as identical twin actors—
Fresh Hollywood discoveries, practicing dialogue.

　It's ironic that Hollywood elites disapprove of
　　Those with conservative-view ideologies.
　The cultural problems that pervade the left coast
Breed riots, drug wars, and assorted garbologies.

　Brendan met elitists who knew more than God,
And brilliant edgy artists addicted to prescriptions.
　Brandon met vegans and issue-oriented activists
And various egotistical weirdoes—of all descriptions.

　Discovering California was an adventurous goal—
Through gridlock, forest fires, mudslides, and quakes.
Though there are traditions like the famed Rose Bowl,
　The film industry thrives on what liberties it takes.

　Since Brandon was a self-professed conservative,
　　The screenings were never offered to him.
　Brendan attended Democratic fundraisers
Wearing flamboyant attire under a pseudonym.

　　It came to pass that Brendan was called—
　He became a rising star at Studio Paramount.
When movies were shot, and traffic was stalled,
　　Brandon showed up on Brendan's account.

They switched and swapped for vital roles
Then an Academy Award was suggested.
Brendan won, and son-of-a-gun, Brandon accepted—
Despite never screening for the role—he never tested.

Averse Again Now and Then

View of Padgett Thomas Barracks, The Citadel, 2009

Chapter Seven

Growth of a Notion

A Response in Wisconsin

There was a clairvoyant from Racine
Who predicted scores of games unseen.
They bet big when the Packers played,
But the game was tape delayed.
She took the cash and flew to St. Augustine.

A bowling-tour bowler from Eau Claire
Won a championship on a seven-ten spare.
He missed it at first,
But when a thunderclap burst,
The tenpin shook down in thin air.

Bellhops in Madison, Wisconsin,
Earn tips from their pleasant responsin'.
They scout the big spenders
Who'd been out on benders,
And notice if they bring a young nuance in.

A former Russian spy walked her Boykin.
She moved to the lakefront after perestroika'n.
She found American free trade
Amenable enough to persuade
Her to leave espionage for a home in Sheboygan.

When the Council Bluffs

There's never been anything quite as raucous
As the way they perform an Iowa caucus.
They meet in every county—each precinct—
And verbalize whatever it is that they think
It's odd their counties are nearly all rectangular
Except for the river-bordered ones, more angular.
They have diversified the state from only farming
And their low rate of crime is quite "disarming."
One can live in Davenport or Council Bluffs—
There's little need for warrants or handcuffs.
If you're considering an Iowa vacation, get goin'.
A Hawkeye State trip begins in Des Moines.

Texas Two-Step

It's the biggest state in the lower forty-eight.
Rhode Island could fit inside Dallas.
They refined the west and the oil was next,
Each oil baron's domain is a palace.

They gave us the Alamo, the Lone Star flag,
And sports teams like the San Antonio Spurs.
From Beaumont going west, it's eight-hundred miles
Before another state other than Texas occurs.

It's far—so far—that if you take your car
You'd run out gas twice trying to cross it.
And if you rented a rental without adding accidental,
You'd be dodging mule deer to keep your deposit.

The Ft. Lauderdale Splash

Statistical data
Shouldn't matta.
Most Floridians
Are amphibians.
They take to water
Like they oughta,
Like sleepy dolphins
On endorphins.
They like to swim—
A synonym
For aquatics,
Like hypnotics
Are drawn
Like a swan
To beach or lake
With subtle wake,
And undeterred
The Snowbirds
Return
As winter adjourns,
To a place up north
Where henceforth
They are Yanks again,
Without disdain—
Awaiting fall—
When they will all
Grow fins anew
As Floridians do.

Albert Kahn

Note Albert Kahn[27]
The architect
Had plans he'd drawn
With much effect.

He placed the line
In walls of glass.
By his design
The cars could pass.

All on one floor—
One direction.
Each tech man's chore—
Each connection!

Old Henry Ford
Had found the way
To nudge toward
The modern day.

Kahn's nuanced plans
Would thus enshrine,
First credit of man's
Assembly line.

Yet we concede
On H. Ford's lawns
Old Henry's deed,
Not Albert Kahn's.[28]

W. Thomas McQueeney

Rooftops of Tallinn, Estonia, 2004

Shakespeare Comes to Walmart

    Arkansas is a proud and fertile state—
Boasting Johnny Cash, Walmart, and Al Green.
    Add in Sonny Liston, champ heavyweight—
        By Texas with Texarkana between.
Called the native People of the South Wind,
Down-home folk from Fort Smith to Little Rock
    Consider themselves hopeful, not chagrinned.
    Dawning Sundays, the fiery preachers talk.
Each fall week presents Fayetteville's showcase—
    Football consumes every Razorback fan—
        Ev'ry ear and eyeball in ev'ry place
    Follows the Hogs' score over a lifespan.
    Gone as memories, a past for squintin'—
    God bless Arkansas, no more clan Clinton.[29]

Mizurah!

In Missouri they don't say Missouri.
They pronounce it "Mizurah" instead.
They mention things unmentionable
With nary an untold word unsaid.
They fashioned a gateway arch at St. Louie
And bake Budweiser into their bread.

It's not surprising in the Show Me State
That performance is the ultimate test.
The irony that Tennessee Williams was born there
Indicates a first name given in jest.
Personalities like Mark Twain and Dizzy Dean
Became examples of Mizurah's best.

There are unbelievable destinations in Mizurah
Like the Ozark Mountains and Branson.
St. Joseph marked the beginning of the Oregon Trail,
It's a state that Lewis and Clark took a chance in.
If you head on down to their Independence home,
You'd find the house the Trumans found romance in.

If you're out that way anyway.
Take a tour-a Mizzurah.

No Maine Tribute Goes Unnoticed

The rain meant for Maine
Falls plainly in Spain.
Snow—it comes again
And again, and again.

It's the hideaway hidden
Away for the mobsters.
Tide tables are a state religion,
And so are Maine lobsters.

Sleepy Kennebunkport
Has entered the world stage
It would have been a last resort,
If not for the forty-first presidential age.

Literary Maine was forlorn
Among Mainer's identity regrets—
Though Longfellow was Portland born,
Maine began as Massachusetts.

Living there, it's scarcely rare
That you hear the north wind stir—
It's coming hard, the "nor'easter."
As the fishermen and the plowmen concur.

The spelling of tribes in history books
Much to the schoolchildren's chagrin,
Note the Passamaquoddy and Arosaguntacook—
Both tribes considered Algonquin.[30]

W. Thomas McQueeney

Maine's legislature meets by resource
Despite winter's frequent snow duster,
No exclusive national golf course
Lies near their capitol of Augusta.

The Pine Tree State has many moose.
(The plural should be meese.)
Maine promotes these mammals to reproduce
And migrate like Canadian geese.

Reindeer used to roam freely in Maine
When the Mainiacs called them Caribou.
Their drift into New Brunswick should explain—
Why they're the stock of New Brunswick Stew.

It remains that the rain meant for Maine
Falls plainly in Spain…or so perhaps…
The snow that comes again and again,
Ceases in summer and they put out lobster traps.

Alabama Ramble

There was a young Roll Tide man in Red Bay
Who said his wife was an angel at twenty-five.
But an Auburn grad from Tuscumbia
Told him he was lucky, 'cause his was still alive.

The highway patrol is strict along I-20.
In a police report found copied by twittering—
They arrested a lady from Tuscaloosa yesterday
Whose dog had puppies there…for littering.

The playhouse stayed full in Birmingham,
Where they showcased five sister acts about puns.
There was no theme to follow they told the crowd—
It was just a play on words made by nuns.

A couple who lost their jobs in Mobile
Said they were laid off instead of being fired.
They had to go without food, shoes, and clothing
Noting that abstinence makes *everything* desired.

The cemetery going west out of Huntsville
Just published an increase of their burial costs.
A priest in a parish near Montgomery noted that
The cost of living and the cost of dying got crossed.

There just ain't no place quite like Alabama—
From Sheffield to Phenix City to Fairhope.
There's barbecue and football and belles of the ball.
If someone's bored there, you've found a misanthrope.

Illini Line Item

There's a silent *S* in Illinois.
It's silent like the *S* in corps.
It's not pronounced the way it's spelt—
One must halt at the last syllable dealt,
And make the noise no more.

There's a silent *S* in Illinois—
The sound creates a sudden void.
Most think its degree of *debris apropos*,
As some *S*s written may never know
When to shut up or to be employed!

Averse Again Now and Then

Cliffs of Moher, Ireland, 2008

Chapter Eight

Manifest Quest

Per Capita

The state of Mississippi has more donors per capita, than
Any other state on the whole map. If a brand of being
Was canned and agreed to be marketed, then people
Of Mississippi would be harvested for their genuineness.
Mississippi also has more churches per capita, and those selfless
People of the Magnolia State search their souls each day
To give away so much to the poor, which is ironic
Because Mississippi has per capita more impoverished folks
Than any state extant. The state is not afraid of a battle either—
Since Mississippians seem made to rattle a saber as in the past,
Which shows more Mississippians per capita died for
The Confederate cause from their caliber of heroics—
And this continued into the First World War, when history
Repeated itself by taking Mississippi's native sons in ratio more
Than all others, per capita. All is a credit to the Mississippi mothers
Who have taught and toiled and set examples of kindness, each
Forthright in their quest to refine best behaviors for the sons
And daughters who took their orders from their elders who
Found that Mississippi, per capita, has held her own, and
Prides itself on inspiring their young to reach without hindrance
Convinced that acquiring knowledge is the entrance to life,
Since the cost of education, per capita,
Will never be as expensive as the cost of ignorance.[31]

The Ballad of the Caesar Salad

The Muncie Gnome Restaurant chef
Never realized he was partially deaf.

While the live band strummed a guitar lick—
A Caesar salad was ordered with extra garlic.

"Three cloves, with mayo and fresh anchovies,"
Came out as "love for you to throw in snow peas."

There are no snow peas in a Caesar salad.
Their presence renders a true Caesar invalid.

With two tablespoons of grated Parmesan cheese,
All Caesars were prepared with his expertise.

Worcestershire sauce, mustard and egg yolk,
Made especially for the munchin' Muncie folk.

Cracked black pepper, with a pinch of routine salt
Made the Indiana epicurean palates cuisinely vault.

Ordering snow peas should ruin a good Caesar,
But the deaf chef allowed it as most hesitant appeaser.

He brought the Caesar bowl and legumes to the orderer.
As the waiter refreshed the bread and poured the water.

The snow peas were a hit, for the surprised customer's sake.
Snow-pea Caesars were Indiana invented by an audacious mistake.

It's Safe to Try the Pralines

There are Spanish, French, and American graves—
All who lent their genes to New Orleans—
As did the Choctaw and the African slaves.

Each contributed to their delectable cuisines.

The Big Muddy runs through it at a turn.
Where ancient cultures dug out their pirogues.
Louisiana is a healthy classroom to learn
The origin and interaction that created their brogues.

The French pronunciations like étouffée and beignet
Were Anglicized and Cajunized into Yat.[32]
It's likely that a visit to the Crescent City may
Have you shake in double takes before saying, "Say what?"

It is recommended that you attend a Cajun festival event,
Where you might have jambalaya so hot you'll steam.

The locals say they'll "berl d'ersters" in heavy accent,
They'll "wirsh de ants all wrinch'd in a zink till cleaned."

An Elegy from Dayton Going South

She said that snow was blocking her drive,
And that her garage door was iced all shut.
She was out of groceries and couldn't decide
If she should leap from a window to walk her mutt?

Her television station just shows old cold news—
No movies, no sports, no fashion shows on.
Her radio broadcasts carry chilling views
Of boring opinions—frosted from dusk to dawn.

Ohio's wintertime weather stays bitterly cold.
Her snowbird neighbors went south to warm up.
But summers in Ohio—bright and bold—
Start lines in the parks where children form up.

From Cincy to Cleveland, Toledo to Kent,
Warm weather in the Buckeye State agrees.
It's when snowbirds' money once Florida spent—
Returns home to Ohio's eighty degrees.

It's best not to gripe about time and place,
Knowing the seasons will forever change.
Just plan for the snowfall and just in case—
A condo in that other Miami can be arranged!

She can walk the mutt near Bal Harbour Mall
Or stroll down the art deco boulevards.
She can drink and party in some Merengue hall,
Or sit on South Beach ogling lifeguards.

Averse Again Now and Then

When spring tips its cap in April or May,
Return to Dayton by making the drive.
Some Ohioan is looking for an Ohio fiancée,
Honk your horn heading north on I-95.

Memphis
451 Miles

It's more than four hundred miles from Knoxville to Memphis.
It's hard to complete the trip in a day.
The best part of driving those four hundred miles is that
Nashville comes along about halfway.

Nashville has an abundance of what most cities envy,
Like an identity for country music's most famous.
They strum the beat of the true cruel romances—
We knew we were art before they framed us.

Tennessee bustles with character from end to end,
Considering it's shaped like a Band Aid Sheer Strip.
The eastern part and the western part are extremes—
They seem to have a distant cousin relationship.

The Volunteer State has beautiful parks and natural sites—
And we haven't even mentioned Chattanooga or Kingsport;
Or Dayton, where the Darwinian teacher John Scopes[33]
Stood the world on trial and was held in contempt of court.

A Vanderbilt study reports Tennesseans walk 902 miles per year,
Or the distance across Tennessee and back by their rationale'n.
Another study noted they each drink twenty-two gallons of alcohol
annually.
Based on these two reports, a Tennessean gets forty-one miles per
gallon.

Snow hills outside of Townsend, Tennessee, 2016

Bluegrass and Green Skies

    Spring breakers from Kentucky leave Kentucky,
    And head south to the most southernmost places.
    They find the best deals on their portable devices
      By manipulating their digital databases.

When really, they'd save much by staying in Paducah,
Because their rates are lower than any hotel in Cancun.
And they might get to enjoy Kentucky's storied history,
A history that boasts the great trailblazer, Daniel Boone.

Dan'l walked nearly everywhere unless he rode on a wagon.
The Wilderness Road wound through the Cumberland Gap—
Places that were both unknown until this frontiersman hero
Went on his own spring break to find hunting places to map.

    Kentucky celebs are Ashley Judd, Loretta Lynn, and George Clooney.
    The Bluegrass State has racing horses, basketball, and Kentucky Fried—
Add Lexington and Louisville, Owensboro, Frankfort and Fort Knox.
Of all that lifts the Bluegrass culture, its bourbon remains its pride.

138

Vermonters Like Who Haiku

Vermont pastoral
Fond of fauna and floral
Quieted quarrel

Barbershop exchange
Heard discussing a state change
To elders it's strange

A need apparent
Purposeful law ran errant
Semitransparent

New legislation
Decriminalization
High protestation

Vermonters want a
Medical marijuana
From dusk to dawn-a

With ballots coming
And Vermonters succumbing
Each barber's humming

Should the potheads jaunt
To the barbers of Vermont
Forget what they want

W. Thomas McQueeney

All barbers abound
Steadfastly hold to their ground
No weed to drag down[34]

Dot the Eye in Island

Rhode Island is not an island,
Though Block Island certainly is.
The slow ferry takes an hour to cross,
Try the hydro-jet boat—it's a whizz!

The smallest state of any state—
But not so its national stature—
They covet ownership seriously there,
If you lose your wife, they'll attach her.

There are only five counties tightly meshed.
Four connect the Narragansett Bay.
The interstate bisects the state in two parts,
Providence is unavoidable in every way.

In Bristol they celebrate July the Fourth
With a parade that is conspicuously led
By a curiously remodeled children's toy
Repurposed as Uncle Sam Potato Head.

Patamechanics Hall—showcases the absurd.
There's a time machine placed within it.
If luck is upon you, jump into the display,
You'll be out of Rhode Island in a minute.

They Got It All

The Tar Heel State has academic fate
Of widespread cultural diversity.
Thou doth not protest a right or a left
Without running into another university.

They got it all in North Carolina.
Every wonder over and under-done.
They have UNC and Duke basketball,
And NASCAR racing's favorite son.

Ava Gardner hailed from Westfield
To become the state's first true starlet.
Don't confuse those Outer Banks
With the inner banks there in Charlotte.

They do great things in technology there.
Ask any Research Triangle-ist.
If one wants to visit an even better place,
Visit Billy Graham, their home evangelist.

No Thanks, Mr. Stuyvesant

Not dizzied, not dazzled, or anything worse
Looking up and all around and down—
They say the center of the universe
Runs from Central Park through the Midtown.

The city is also the name of the state,
Confusing senses tend to cluster.
The state of mind refers to the cityscape,
As if the New York upstate were lackluster.

There's Syracuse and Schenectady,
Places Mr. Stuyvesant would've likely lauded.
No one knows whether he traveled there,
Though the upstate is summarily applauded.

The Big Apple has an abrupt attitude.
Their braggadocio is expletive-driven.
The sounds emit horrific amplitude,
It's a hell of a place to work and live in.

W. Thomas McQueeney

View of Lake Santee, 2012

Chapter Nine

Declaration of Interdependence

Poca-Honey

Jamestown was established in 1607.[35]
Neither you nor I experienced being there.
If we had asked Princess Pocahontas for a date—
She would've likely found one of us debonair.

Let's imagine her a femme of native beauty
With dark rivulets of hair down her back.
She certainly would have been quite curious
Should our pickup line have cited a sign in the zodiac.

Maybe we could have coyly approached her
By impressing her that we both owned a Ferrari.
We could've enticed her with a trip to Vegas,
Or even dangled to her a guided African safari.

Surely she would have been enamored
By the platinum coating on our credit cards—
Or the chauffeur waiting to whisk us away
Amid our uniformed personal bodyguards.

Come to think of it, you might not be single.
So her choice of mates would not include thee.
But if I were part of the 1607 Jamestown time,
I'd wonder why she decided upon John Rolfe, not me.

Rolfe had none of Captain John Smith's valor,
Nor would he have had my legendary largesse.
It's likely that she selected John Rolfe because
He was the first settler who taught her to say yes.

Barnacle Geese and Bobwhites

Where would one find
A kaleidoscope of fall—
Hearty and airish—
The smell of hickory firewood,
An evening for a shawl,
Clam chowder
And nutmeg powder,
Coffee for conversations
Begun in warmth,
Friendly neighbors—
Softened salutations;
A hearth—
Across a valley
Laden with snow
Melting to a drizzle,
Nature's yawn—
Aperitif swizzle,
A fawn appears—
Sensual release,
Barnacle geese and bobwhites?
Starlights,
Quiet nights.

An idyllic dream—
That's for damn sure.
Consciousness streamed—
Visit New Hampshire.

Fellows of the Palmettos

There's pride of living in the Palmetto State—
The smallest in the southern region.
Since the introduction of Deep Woods Off,
The mosquitoes can no longer lay siege in.

There's mountains that overlook South Carolina,
And rivers and lakes and hydroelectric dams.
In Aiken they raise racing horses for races,
In Camden, they dress as messieurs and mesdames.

More peaches are grown in the peach belt upstate
Than in all of Georgia combined.
At Greenville, they reinvigorated the downtown streets
For a new Carolina state of mind.

Myrtle Beach is a Grand Strand playground treat.
Hilton Head has more heads than Hiltons—
And Columbia houses an odd legislature
In offices opulent with bars and built ins.

The Lowcountry extends to barrier islands
With golf courses, tennis courts, and croquet.
Head there by maps with no purpose or reason
And never a cause to return from the island causeway.

The crown-jewel destination of the state of Palmettos
Is the founding city on a harbor wide and deep.
Charleston is the Holy City of tall church spires.
Arrive there with cash to spare, the rooms ain't cheap!

W. Thomas McQueeney

If you're passing through on two-lane ninety-five,
And you have no plans to stay and visit—
You may change your mind when the traffic backs up;
You'll think it's a bad wreck, but is it?[36]

Mixed Lexicon on the Eastern Shore

Lawrence E. Mulligan of the Eastern Shore
Tried to make it as an orator out west.
There was nothing Lawrence wanted more
Than to speak eloquently at his very best.

By latent dyslexia Lawrence was troubled.
He could not read or recite his correspondence.
Some letters disappeared or doubled,
His eyes twisted his brain to despondence.

He saw signs on the highway that read Etix (not)—
Like the place to buy seats for concerts.
Another at the intersection seemed to say Spot.
Like the stains on his ties and shirts.

He made it to Fran Sandisco and Torf Worth
And then to Lake City Salt and Vast Legos.
He filled the forums with his verbal mirth,
But couldn't tell the word *soggy* from Eggos.

Lawrence squinted to read the words he wrote,
His serious speeches came off as if he were a comedian.
His dyslexia meant words could stick in his throat,
Though the Palmer method detailed a most legible pen.

He stopped in Moribalt as he arrived back in Maryland,
And contemplated a future as he munched on barc cakes.
He asked the waiter if he said words he could understand—
The waiter replied that all mankind is full of mistakes.

This inspired him to enter the seminary and become a priest.
He memorized holy audiotapes for each Sunday homily.
His life found order in his church on the Shore of the East—
His orations still dyslexilized; his clarity was an anomaly.

Father Mulligan had traveled both near and wide,
And had overcome much of his vernacular affliction.
Though a funeral or Holy Mass could often backslide—
He'd voice "fools encryption" instead of "crucifixion."

Where *R* the R's?

There are differences denounced
As Pilgrims and Puritans are confused—
Both are followers of John Calvin,
But one faction has never used
The noose or burning at the stake,
When women were brutally abused.

The initiators of the revolution gathered—
J. Adams, J. Hancock and P. Revere.
Add in Massachusetts's literary legends—
Whistler and Whitney and Whittier.
The Bay State gave Emerson and Dickinson—
Our language became light and prettier.

A British colony no longer Brit
It's a long retreat to the Berkshires.
Elm trees line Brookline streets,
A chill chills the haut coutures.
Exit left only, there is no right;
The Bay Colony took many detours.

Boston, the major port occurs
By a bay and a cape and a sea.
The ruling British claimed it
With their tax upon colonial tea.
It's now where the American
Tea Party would least likely be.

More French lineagers reside there
Than from all the places in Britain.

Italians passed the Brits and French
It was easier for Italians to get in.
But none of the cultures can compare
With the heritage the Irish have written.

Colleges steeped in privilege—
Harvard, MIT, BC, and Wellesley.
High society's steps are higher yet
Where whatever compels ye or thee
To honor Massachusetts etiquette—
To suggest, redress, and protest me.

They grow traffic jams across MA state,
And brewpubs grow faster than corner bars.
Which brings us to the Big Dig subway system—
Because Boston loathed those gridlocked ca's.
The workers dug deep knowing they couldn't keep
Their forefather's remnants—their missing *R*s.

Averse Again Now and Then

Boy Thomas and puppy Maggie, 2003

Connecticut at Night

Connecticut has ominous haunts
Not bars or clubs or restaurants.
One is wise to avoid and fear its
Notoriously scary ghostly spirits.

In Derby's Opera House, Sterling—
Cries at dawn are blood curdling.
Heed Bridgeport's Remington Arms,
Where who knows who sets the alarms.

Union Cemetery rises in quiet Easton,
Where the pale woman is deceased in.
Dudleytown in Cornwall is vacant
Everybody died, goblins awakened.

In the Mansfield Training School,
Mental patients have turned to ghoul.
The New London Ledge Light drifts—
Though abandoned, it still has shifts.

Many are paranoid of the paranormal—
In headless bodies, bloody informal.
Thus you're warned by haunting etiquette,
Go by day, not by night to Connecticut.[37]

An Ode to Georgia

It was Sherman, William Tecumseh,
An ominous soldier of contempt—
Who at Central Park invokes kumbaya—
But in Atlanta is rebuked as soul exempt.
His glory grew by his inhumanity
At the expense of death, fire, and obliteration—
As he rose within the celebration of carnage-vanity.
The cause which caused a re-creation
Re-created. Debated.
Decades of Atlantans toiled unadvanced
And by and by,
A new Atlanta was enhanced.

Historians trend a victor's deeds,
With tacit imbalance;
A winner succeeds—
They are pseudo blessed, imbued with talents;
Speakers at banquets,
Heroes to youth;
Laurels cast full like blankets
Never quite reconciling truths.
And what is written unchallenged becomes in bronze
Bas-relief attached to polished marble icons.

Now, as the world is information heightened,
And since access is universal—
The public consciousness becomes enlightened,
And the prevailing sentiment merits reversal:
But the result, despite Sherman's intent,

Cannot be denied.
The resolve of the Georgians remained unbent
A tattered leadership stepped into the chasm to guide.
An Atlanta that would become exemplary—

Without contempt extemporaneously.
The crossroads of the new southern miracle,
An Atlanta that was felled by Sherman, but would remember he
Was never human, but to them demonically mythical—
And the state that surrounded,
Came forward to embolden
The New South duly crowned
In a new age golden.

So it is that General William Tecumseh Sherman
Changed Atlanta, changed Georgia,
And every southern state.
A region that knew his ire and wrath
Was at once determined
To rise, rebuild, to forge a higher fate.

When curious students attended
The University of Georgia to get a history degree,
They found that General Sherman recommended
A scorched-earth policy on his march to the sea.
There were unspeakable crimes, many starved,
All indecencies allowed in the name of war.
Sherman's fiery path was carved
So that Savannah would heed its destiny in store.

Averse Again Now and Then

They could find nothing remarkable about the general
Nothing to lift the heart
No insight to impart—
Except that Sherman died in the dark,
Not at his home, but in New York.
His corpse was sent to St. Louis by train
And was delivered home there in steady rain.
Sherman was buried there
Amidst the accolades and fanfare.

It should be noted further,
That the 1958 St. Louis Hawks—
Champions of the National Basketball Association—
Later, despite vitriolic banter,
Broke off negotiations and talks.
They opted amid much fervor
To move to Atlanta.

Urban Crawl

Princeton, Rutgers, Seton Hall,
Fairleigh Dickinson, and even Rider.
New Jersey colleges in urban sprawl
Are expanding ever wider.

Princeton is in Princeton.
Trenton has Rider U.
Rutgers and Seton Hall
You'd see in Newark passing through.

Fairleigh Dickinson University
Owns two campus lawns to mow.
They're more spread out than anyone—
Like an educational traveling show.

People rave about the education system—
New Jersey has well-prepared youth.
Note the most popular structure for getting there
Is the garden variety Garden State tollbooth.

Kite Flying 101
A Tribute to Ben Franklin

The lightning rod
From chimney to sod
Saved lives
And archives
In public libraries
With diaries
And almanacs.
Smokestacks
From his stoves,
The treasure troves
Of maxims,
And French madams
Protected by the rod
Interconnected the demigod
The Quaker
Peacemaker
Serving as a diplomat
An anti aristocrat
Inventor of the bifocal
And the local
University
Within his diversity
He edited a constitution
With simple elocution.
When it comes to Renaissance men,
Think of Gentleman Ben.

Delawares on You

Herschel registered his yacht in Dover.
Then Wilmington billed his credit card.
But Herschel lives well outside the first state,
He's a yachter swayed by the avant-garde.

There's a twelve-mile-circle border in Delaware.
It created a wedge once called no-man's-land.
Some claimed it as Philadelphia's new basement,
But Delaware grabbed it by "first" demand.

The DuPonts provided the state's industry giant
So this little colony could compete and persevere.
Herschel registered his yacht through the post office,
But never moored it anyplace north of Cape Fear.

It's a conundrum that Delawareans
Extend their commerce by email and faxes.
And by allowing interstate improprieties
Like registering yachts without resident taxes.

You could walk all of Delaware in a day or two.
You could fly its length during a TV commercial.
But if you really want to see the best side of Delaware,
Locate the return address for the yachtsman Herschel.[38]

Decency, Descent, and DC

Should visitors swoon? Washington or Washingtoon?
Sworn adversity, darkened perversity.
Amazing universities!
A conspiracy, a cathartic city, or a commune?

There's four hundred thirty-five in the House;
Another hundred in the Senate.
They give the lobbyists favors—many misbehavers,
They take our money and carelessly spend it.

Cherry-blossom flowers. Separation of powers.
Wide National Mall;
An obelisk tall;
Innumerable conflicts of interest after hours.

Debt ain't funny; the treasury prints money
Smithsonian museums galore
Oval Office, rectangular door.
Crossing many bridges to land of milk and honey.

Nine justices in nine robes. Some ideological homophobes.
City disquieting,
Marches and rioting—
Running out of allies and alienating friends on our globe.

A lonely resident is a two-term president.
Demands beyond a salary;
National Portrait Gallery;
National Cathedral for each rare blessed event.

The Capitol's strange and records each exchange—
From *I*s to *R*s to *D*s.
Hearing these, we ask God, please—
Grant me the serenity to accept what we can never change!

Averse Again Now and Then

Teddy bear and car keys, a time passage, 2012

Chapter Ten

Alpaca Llama and You Bring the Jaguar

Hurts My Ears

I curiously ask, "What is it with what it is?"
The worst cussing I ever got was from a teenager named Liz.
She bumped my Smart Car when I had the audacity
To change lanes to the lane she wanted with hyper tenacity.

My car was there and her car was not
Until she forced herself upon my spot.
She was late for school and her trunk stereo blared.
She was texting her friends and acting weird.

I heard words never uttered by the most drunken sailor.
I yearned for the police to arrive, perhaps they'd jail her.
She was ticketed for the accident she obviously triggered
But not for the language she tossed, scorned, and sniggered.

She couldn't get through a phrase without a curse,
And each sentence led to another sentence worse.
There was obscenity, blasphemy, and utterances profane—
Hurling epithets, insults, and expletives she could not constrain.

She became quiet a moment and pulled from her wallet—
Her license, her registration, and an earbud set to install it.
She plugged them into her smartphone near my Smart Car crunched up
And chilled to a rapper's rap while the rubberneck traffic bunched up.

She began rapping to the beat and spouting the rapper phrases,
Running through profanity's worst while upset drivers glared gazes.

She learned all of her vocabulary by embracing the rapper's jam
And I was left with a sultry teen, a traffic cop, and a reason for an epigram.

Learning the use of proper language is a mighty intellectual pursuit.
There are 470,000 words in an unabridged dictionary to elocute.
The brain remembers those most repeated as we daily converse—
Why not fill it with words that paint our dreams, instead of the perverse?

Many of the words of vulgarity are senseless hyphenated conjunctions—
That, taken as described, direct ridiculous and absurd physical functions.
Their boisterous use convinces most onlookers and eyewitnesses
To deduce that the user is unfit for polite society, among other unfitnesses.[39]

Social Media

Evan railed against owning a beeper
His beeping children were not thrilled.
It caused them considerable frustration
Evan was not giving in; he was strong willed.

"I'm not living my life for your convenience,"
Evan to his kids casually explained.
"I do not want to be available twenty-four seven!"
From the beeper culture, Evan abstained.

Beepers gave way to cellular phones,
And Evan's children again approached.
"This is yet another interruption for your ease.
My personal time will not be broached."

In time the smartphone was invented.
It added features too tempting to ignore.
So Evan bought the finest new version
When iPhone 3 became iPhone 4.

He found quotes for stock on his camera phone—
Evan was hooked and added more apps.
He took no calls from his invasive children—
Preferring YouTube, GPS, and Google Maps.

A fair solution was offered by his kids—
One that would not make their dad become vexed.
They offered to show him how to block messages,
If he would agree to accept their texts.

So Evan agreed to the new correspondence
And said he'd lift his self-imposed ban.
But the first time each of them texted their dad
His reply came back that his dad was over his dad-a plan!

Nuptials Disrupted

Romeo and Juliette had the medieval hots,
But never married through five acts, ersatz…
Marriage is for those of blinded faith
Like Elizabeth Taylor and Henry the Eighth.

A license, a blood test, and a fancy diamond
Provide legitimacy that benefits social climbin'.
Two lovers would remain true lovers if
The stench of marriage had a warning whiff.

Combining the bills and the checking account
Always leads to a smaller balance amount.
When one and one are permanently two
"For poorer, for worse" much sooner comes true.

If accidents arrive as lads and lasses,
Save for costly colleges, braces, and glasses.
There will be in-laws likely that nobody likes.
Soft concerns grow fast into hardened gripes.

By accepting two as one before the altar
Sets a sure prognosis that both will falter.
Changes in expected routines require repentance,
Marriage is a word that becomes a sentence.

The Crematorium Comes to the Top

There was an open-house event at the crematorium.
Urns were displayed beside the hors d'oeuvres.
Most customers attended out of courtesy,
Though some admitted to frazzled nerves.

The parking area was full of expensive cars—
The backyard ambiance warmed by tiki torches.
The gas lamps that lined the front walkway
Led everyone to breezy candlelit porches.

Pricing brochures were subtly indiscreet,
And the chatter was void of the usual dictums.
The party reached its most abrupt hysteria
When the host announced discounts to burn victims.

Dove Story

Lovesick Hector stepped near the ledge,
And as he inched toward the outer edge.
His dream girl dashed his wedding plans
By late entertaining her many fans.

The jilted suitor had climbed to the roof
With a bottle of spirits, ninety proof.
There, he became momentarily captured—
A dove and a pigeon were enraptured.

The birds paid no attention to Hector
Who had invaded their lofty sector.
The pigeon had the dove fully wooed.
As she coquettishly and coyly cooed.

Their flighted love was first sighted
Near the heights where they alighted.
They were dovetailed and pigeon-toed,
He arranged his twigs for her abode.

But Hector had made the full ascension
Without coddling the bird's attention.
He was determined to vault ahead
Falling to his death until fully dead.

A pigeon grunts expecting lovely coos—
His mating sound among majestic views.
The romance reminded the would-be jumper
That he should move on and simply dump her.

Summerall Chapel at The Citadel, 2014

Judgment

What I did, I did.
What it was, it was.
Headed home, God forbid—
He will do as He does.
Left unto fate,
Hope He can wait.

Frontier Fantasy

The lovely young girl bedded where
Her deerskin hide hid the frontier.
She was thankful for her warming gear,
And to the chief who had killed the deer.

The aging chief was sagely seditious—
His luxurious bearskin quite inauspicious.
His visionary dream of youthful wishes—
Was tribally thought of as overly ambitious.

One night on the plains, it was windy and damp.
When the pretty Native American vamp
Took the warmth of her flickering fire lamp—
Intent on seducing the chief, she made camp.

The chief did what chiefs don't condone.
The tribe could not force the chief to atone.
The morning dew found them cuddled alone—
On their bearskin and deerskin, covers blown!

Cemetery Signs

Stones and pillars and mausoleums;
Romantically natural outdoor museums—
Lives described by dates and surnames,
Countless immortalities with counterclaims.
An array of characters who no longer roam
Unto eternal rest are inscribed to their last home.

There are murderers, monks, and Presbyterians,
Pharmacists, cellists, and Shakespeareans.
There are college graduates and retired dentists,
Professional counselors, who had once apprenticed.
There are leftists, cads, poets, and the Mafioso.
Socialites, Mennonites, and the grandioso.

Just over by the live oak is a grave being dug.
Awaits the box of a sap awaiting a miracle drug.
He invested in research, with millions for science—
His last rites fulfilled, a church and mortuary alliance.
The tent will hold family, and his partner-innovator.
No miracles for the partner either, his funeral will come later.

The Boracle of Wi-Fi

They assumed he was a professor because
He awed and amazed all of the patrons.
He posed conundrums to the students gathered,
And gave parenting advice to the matrons.

The punkish girl Ruth with the orange hair
Grudgingly made his lattés to serve him.
Her crude declaration that he was a bore
Did nothing to dissuade or unnerve him.

He surfed the web for innocuous facts.
He sensed all the senses surrounded.
When lightning struck the coffee shop,
His sensory gifts were at once expounded.

His American Express read "Eliot Toile."
His parents preferred a palindromic name.
He spouted the capitals of every world country
But called the punk girl "whatshername."

One day the elderly Professor Toile
Failed to come in for his morning latté.
The orange-haired girl, unconcerned and distant,
Didn't miss the old man's luminous cachet.

They said he passed when Halley's Comet
Crossed the heavens at the Belt of Orion.
There was no chatter at the café that day—
When Eliot Toile died, the café began dying.

Averse Again Now and Then

He was a wealthy man and left a curious will.
    It was to be read aloud at his booth.
It gave millions to those who asked for his help,
    But only his last tip to orange-haired Ruth.

The café nearly closed the following winter
    The counter sales couldn't be bolstered.
But there in his booth was a gift for Ruth
    Concealed in the seat she re-upholstered.

An envelope lay flat under the cushion where he sat
Marked "Ruth" and began with the word, "Whereby"
    Inside it read, "This bearer bond's for you.
"Cash it in, and go and buy yourself some hair dye."

Owen Cohen

Owen Cohen used to have an issue with authority
But that issue was authoritatively resolved.
Before that, he had an awful argument with his spouse,
After which she became otherwise involved.

Owen Cohen made so much money betting on football
That he tidily concealed all his winnings away.
But alas, he could not resist the irresistible—
And lost his entire winnings on one single play.

His bar tab was tabulated at the local pub—
An amount he had no immediate means to settle.
He was punched in the nose before going home—
Intruding upon where he ought not mettle.

His rent, his debt, his utilities, and his alimony
Became consequences for the constable's arrival.
When Owen Cohen became significantly overweight,
It impaired his health—and thus—his mortal survival.

Owen Cohen found an answer to fit all of his previous issues—
Leaving his finances askew and other personal solutions undone.
He decided to become an incorrigible and defiant alcoholic—
This way, he combined all of his previous setbacks into just one!

Alpaca Llama and You Bring a Jaguar

Toucan play down the South American way,
Anaconda mentioned the chinchilla.
Tamarin them as their piranha want us to.
A capybara's a rat that looks like Godzilla.

Alpaca llama and you bring a jaguar.
We'll tapir anteater and maybe sip ocelot.
Caiman, condor weasel try to copyu?
We hoped tarantula macaw, but got caught.[40]

Empirical Balance

The Brits claimed land in the Antarctic
Even though it was icy permafrost.
For centuries, they depended on territory gained
As a way of balancing territory lost.

They relinquished Antigua and Barbuda—
Brunei, Saint Kitts and Nevis left.
Trinidad and Tobago flew the coup—
They considered the Grenadines a theft.

The Brits gave up whole continents
Like Australia and North America.
Their diplomats and plenipotentiaries
Were outside the whispered esoterica.

The Brits decreed freedom to Fiji,
To Malta, Cyprus, and New Guinea;
They kept the actors who played worldly roles
Like Alec Guinness and Albert Finney.

They reserved the Cayman Islands,
St. Bart's, Bermuda, and Anguilla.
It gave the queen warm places for tanning
When she was pasty white and vanilla.

All the land the British claimed
When they heralded no setting sun—
Cannot warm up their freezing scientists
In Antarctica where it's minus forty-one.

Averse Again Now and Then

Ft. Lauderdale beach near Miami, 2009

Chapter Eleven

Another Deity in Paradise

Rumors

If a fiction gets traction,
The unfortunate action
Is that seemingly small stuff
Will build friction enough
To fraction a faction.

Tuscarora Jack

An adventurous man from Dublin
Arrived in service to the crown.
He led expeditions to three states
To put all Indian uprisings down.

He went to confront the Tuscarora
In a battle that rendered his name.
And fought the Yemassee at Pocotaligo.
The result was much of the same.

To Darien he trekked with muskets
And built a fort to promote the trades.
He defended against the Creek Muscogee—
Effecting suppression from Indian raids.

From Charleston to Beaufort they knew him,
One of Dublin's finest exports ever.
Tuscarora Jack Barnwell made safe travel
From town to town his lasting endeavor.

To My Fudge Mental Friends

There was a gloomy time when
The comfort I thought I knew
Had reversed and turned again.
They assumed my life askew,
And assessed that I was through.

Erstwhile long-term childhood friends
Whispered unfound awful tales
Through blurred and distorted lenses—
That delighted in blighted details.
The silent call for truth had failed.

By the time the rumors ceased,
New and truer friends emerged.
The most had become the least.
Faith in humanity surged—
Contemptuousness was purged.

Hard lessons place life adrift—
Upon the muddy trail we trudge.
True friends are life's best gifts,
Never give them reasons to judge—
To my judgmental friends–no grudge.

Mercy Margot

Millionaire Margot found the doctor's office,
But lost her parked car in the lot.
Her grandchildren said she was suffering dementia,
But she insisted she was certainly not.

She said she had the shingles,
Pre angina, pre cancer, and pre diabetes
And other ailments that sworn doctors swore
To heal by the name of Hippocrates.

She said she fell victim to a complex—
A foreboding sense of doom.
She hesitated to fill out her medical history
Waiting on death in the waiting room.

Her visit came with a prescription—
Each night prescribed to take two pills.
Margot was rather suspicious about her future—
The pharmacy bottle read "no refills."

With just thirty days of tablets to consume—
And just a month to face her bitter end,
Millionaire Margot took up with a faith healer,
With whom the rest of her life she would spend.

Meeting in a Tornado

We're many miles apart—
Disdainful, but smart—
Distrustful enemies in time.
We're strange bedfellows—
Purples and yellows—
A most begrudging paradigm.

We claim the moral high ground—
Red and white and brown—
Each unlikely to be persuaded.
Considering viewpoints condescending,
Our fences need mending.
We're irrationally, irrevocably jaded.

We can't hear each other
By words that tend to smother
The chance to reach an accord.
We retreat further apart,
While within each other's heart,
We've left understanding unexplored.

This is the story of us—
In religion, race, and thus
Unsolvable barriers are created.
Our tunneled ideologies
Make no apologies.
We waste our lives agitated.

Averse Again Now and Then

There are no words to say
Without a scornful sway
To attempt to bridge the gap.
In derisive tones
Each to each bemoans
The day that started the flap.

If a communist sat with a scientist
And a violinist brought in an atheist—
They'd stay in room and get drunk,
Until the tornado passed them by.
Then they'd herald a cleared-up sky.
And wouldn't care what each other thunk.

No Luck Whatsoever

As an attestation to those timid souls who live timidly
and take no chances—
They do not know risk and reward and never find what romance is.
They never walk under ladders, scaffolding, or broken street lamps,
Or turn off at the exit the wrong way and back up on the on-ramps.

James bought himself a retirement house on a lake near a
hill in a grove.
He was trying to get away by getting lost where others
lost never drove.
But lo and behold one day from the sky dipped a camera attached
to a drone—
And James was discovered uncovered unclothed in a place where
that's uncondoned.

He thought the sign on the gate said it was a colony for those called
"naturists."
He thought he'd rid himself of the curious, the voyeurs, and the
naked insatiarists.
But it was not a sign for nature or for the unnatural, but rather,
"naturalists" it spelled.
The woods had bird watchers, elk photographers—and ogled at
otters they held.

The red-faced James was shown in all his glory to the
local boring press.
He had been seeking refuge at a place where he thought it was okay
to undress.

Averse Again Now and Then

James was a guy who had retired because he was tired of never taking risks,
And now he was facing a female judge looking down at where the breeze was brisk.

She gave him a small fine and a probation and told him he should buy binoculars,
And ordered the clerk to get a towel or a hat or a jock for his exposed joculars.
James never married, never dared to engage, and never accepted advances to even date.
It was precisely because he had no faith in himself and no confidence at all in his fate.

The judge had only the one adjudged case that day in court to render judgment upon,
And directed the constable who directed the drone to lend his tie to James to slip on.
James had a home he bought for a song and lived alone in a grove by the lake.
With a nudge, the female judge took him home hoping he could be her new beefcake.

View of Willemstad, Curacao, 2007

Ned Niblick

"Aye, Ned, you're away, my good man."
The others laughed at something hilarious.
Ned was nearly out-of-bounds.
The mood and the lie were precarious.

A skull preceded a shank to the rough
The casual water was casually found.
He faded the next to the beach with his cleek,
Leaving a chance for an up and down.

The wind whipped the flag to mimic the frenzy.
His partner by the apron had scowled.
"Aye, Ned, you're still away, my friend."
His niblick was cautiously toweled.

From the bunker came a mighty hack
The sphere was cast low from the blade.
It zoomed across the green to an unknown fate,
As the unsteady Ned had again swayed.

A cautious bet was made before the tee
Between Ned's partner and Ned's opponents.
Ned had played so poorly that day—
On the last hole he could make some atonements.

"Double or nothing" was the secret wager
Meaning Ned had to score seven or less.
Ned didn't know what they were laughing about
When they were counting his strokes at address.

W. Thomas McQueeney

He walked up to assess his next buried shot
It sat low in a mangled grass divot.
"Ned, stay down and follow through on this,
And hinge your wrists at the pivot."

The tips were sound and the swing was solid.
The ball sought the hole as an omen.
But poor Ned got the yips and missed the short putt.
His partner put him down for a snowman.

No One to Watch Over

Sharp-minded Addie thinks as if she were younger,
Her unrenewed driver's license says she's actually seventy-nine.
Her mornings became like those old hangovers she had long ago—
They're more painful now—a flaw in life's design.

Her daughter said she was lazy and napped all day,
But Addie preferred to say it was energy efficiency.
Beautiful old people are like great works of art—
A blessing to their children by their self-sufficiency.

Addie was scolded for wearing rumpled clothing,
And never throwing away the old books that she read.
Her daughter said she ought to toss the many volumes away
Because she was sure to do so when Addie was dead.

Addie reads fairy tales to the Saturday children
Who come to the library to hear each melodrama.
She imitates facial expressions of odd-faced characters,
And pauses at each exclamation point, period, and comma.

An Uber driver takes her to serve the soup kitchen;
Another septuagenarian shares her ride to church.
On Mondays she volunteers to answer the phones
At the Community Institute for Cancer Research.

She takes yoga classes on Tuesdays at the senior center
As a way to mingle and meet her aging cronies.
She rides the bus to see her two grandnieces
Receive their certificates at their awards ceremonies.

Her daughter stopped by her flat unannounced,
To bring their longstanding disagreements to a crest.
But Addie had walked to a whiskey bar that afternoon
To enter a ten-million-dollar national trivia contest.

Panicked at her absence, the daughter alarmed the police.
Addie was thought to have been kidnapped—or worse.
Her perfect answers won her the national first prize payout!
Addie moved to Key Largo with her ten-million-dollar purse.

Is WWW about Wrestling?
How Technology Took a Lifetime Vocabulary Away

Grandchildren may find confusing impressions
In our everyday use of archaic expressions.

Like what a "handle" in our lifetime became—
Before it was a grab; now it's a screen name.
A ping always came together with a pong.
Now we ping to reach out and get along.
A profile was once a sideways silhouette.
Now it's a cyber person whose stats we wanna get.
A tablet once had dozens of lines for writing.
Imagine: a touchscreen with variable lighting.
A text was the essence of a schoolbook hardbound.
LOL! It's a verb, used with fewer verbs around.
What was once an entire encyclopedia
Is miniscule to any smartphone's media.
Birds were associated with a sound—a tweet
It's one-forty characters allowed to complete.
If one were to block, it helped the team score.
Now it's for junk mail you don't want anymore.
The cloud was something we saw looking up.
It's even more nebulous now, an information backup.
Google is what we did when we saw pretty lasses.
We Google now for information from the masses.

We may disappear one day from a viral strain like Andromeda,
But they'll just think we're viral like a major YouTube phenomena.

Judith's Walk 2011. [Oil on canvas]

The Pacifist Pugilist

Phil Gist was personally a pacifist
Who learned to be a pugilist.
At Golden Gloves he won his class—
They billed him as Phil the Brass.

But the sportswriters failed to note or list
That Phil was passively a pacifist.
They never could quite reconcile
Why Phil was given an Olympic Trial.

Phil was engaged to Bernice Freeman
She knew Phil had not exorcised his demon.
He had settled much with his righty fist—
Bernice knew this was not the real Phil Gist.

A burly Boston boxer named Harken Gose
Was to topple Phil Gist before going to pros.
The match found Phil weaving and bobbing
While Harken Gose was jabbing and jobbing.

The rounds rolled by, the fourth to the fifth,
Harken Gose sparred at a punchless monolith.
A Massachusetts hook followed an uppercut—
Phil Gist was down with both eyes shut.

The judge, the trainer, and the referee
Noted a quiver when the count made it to three.
By the time they tallied just past eight,
The Brass shot up from his canvassed fate.

W. Thomas McQueeney

He tapped his gloves and peddled back.
When Gose charged in, he gave him a whack.
The aggressor floated left to deliver a blow,
But Phil Gist was waiting to steal the show.

Harken Gose spit out his wet mouthpiece,
Then shouted an insult that mentioned Bernice.
Phil Gist, the passively pacifist pugilist
Made sure Gose's nose didn't move past his fist.

Harken Gose was down and the count began—
Gist in a neutral corner, a much-enraged man.
When the count reached nine, Gist's towel flew.
A certain TKO winner, Gist gave his demon its due.

He retired from boxing and took up a cause
That didn't need tape, smelling salts, or gauze.
The passively pacifist pugilist Phil Gist
Joined a commune and became a commune-ist.

A Blithering Idiot

It was at the Dallas Airport that per chance
Randy ran into an old high school romance.
Louise was a girl who society had dropped out—
She was a de facto whacko, her sanity in doubt.

She was addicted to the smell of wild mushrooms.
Which landed her in institutions without plush rooms.
She liked unconventional things like raising goats—
She knitted her future while sewing her wild oats.

The years that passed were years that she dithered.
She blathered and babbled, piffled and blithered.
Randy noticed her blank stare before asking her for coffee.
Her meds were out, and her appearance looked awfully.

He tried to redirect her to her flight's luggage claim.
She blurted she knew his face but forgot her own name.
Randy tried to escape the awkwardness somehow.
She refused his effort saying she had to scream right now!

The airport security rushed to this odd disturbance—
She told them that Randy was her last known urgence.
Randy told the police that the woman had lost a screw.
A former flame, Lovable Louise had become a Lulu.

They took her in a straightjacket straight to a home.
Where mushrooms grew and goats could roam.
The years that passed were years that she dithered.
She blathered and babbled, piffled and blithered.

Chapter Twelve

Heretic, There a Tick

Penny Ann the Dreamer

A sculptor sculpted Penny Ann the dreamer—
The lithe and lusty model all men craved.
Cloaked in a flowing gown, they deemed her
A perfect femme figure for all time; it's saved.
She sits in chiseled marble by a lighted fountain.
Unto the ages the tall temptress is engraved.
The marble was carried down from the mountain.
The artist pre selected it from the quarry.
The truck man delivered it to the ground in
Blankets of wool wedged into his lorry.
People who passed it saw that the artist
Captured her smile as she stood in her glory.
Town-square models never work so hard as
Penny Ann the dreamer—she wasn't the smartest.[41]

View of Lowcountry marsh near Folly Beach, 2012

Putting Lyrica to Lyrics

Folks never hear the word *pregabalin* anymore.
Come to think of it, most had never heard of it before.
It was used in the advent and proliferation of miracle drugs
With all of its disclaimers, sold on constant television plugs.

Pregabalin was given the mellifluous name *Lyrica*—
A name that is sound pleasing and related to poetica.
It's yet another expensive prescription drug made by Pfizer.
One might forget what it relieves without a chemical advisor.

Pfizer spent millions to develop a counter to fibromyalgia,
With side effects you won't miss with even the worst of nostalgia.
Taking the drug can cause death by a dozen allergic reactions
Like swelling the face, mouth, lips, gums and other distractions.

A user can contract a rash, hives, blisters, or suicidal thoughts,
Depression, restlessness, anxiety, anger, aggression,
but not liver spots.
It can bring on mood swings, agitation, violence,
and trouble sleeping—
Irritability, dangerous impulses, self-harm,
and uncontrollable weeping.

The Lyrica warnings continue from a list of the most ominous listing—
Swelling of hands, legs and feet—and things like conditions pre existing.
Consider getting sick and feverish, drowsiness and blurry visions.
It's best to suffer fibromyalgia rather than suffer the Lyrica provisions![42]

The Nexus of the Sixties

Someone gave out free love,
But Harry was not in the line.
Then they burned their draft cards—
Harry was duty-bound to decline.

At the Haight-Ashbury beat corner,
Where Harry sampled whiskies,
There were free drugs passed around
Amid the nexus of the sixties.

He was on his way out of Frisco
On a frigate to Southeast Asia.
He said goodbye to wife Melinda—
And her flowerchild Anastacia.

Beatles were beating out more tunes
As so were the Rolling Stones.
Harry was gone a year and a half
Amid a divide of racial overtones.

He came back through Manila
And cruised under the Golden Gate.
What love that he had left before
Had turned into violent hate.

If this story seems too serious,
It was not meant to be so.
Melinda was waiting with Anastacia
In Harry's old El Camino.

Harry and Melinda lived happily beyond
With Anastacia happier yet.
If you're ever run over by a nexus,
It makes memories easier to forget!

It's Not What You Think

It may have been a drunken dream,
Or a restless night with sleep apnea—
Or possibly a sleep walk into the woods
Lost on the trails of Appalachia.

Mercy! I'd sighted the hidden entrance!
Eden, that perfect place, was found.
There was so much revelation to savor,
And a mindset that was sure to astound.

There were no pearls on the gates at all.
Just jasmine and honeysuckle entwined.
St. Peter was tweeting his Twitter account.
Any drifting soul was welcome, if inclined.

There were apples to pick all over the place,
And ice cream and tarts and chocolate crepes.
Eden had every delicious taste to sample.
You could eat all you want; but not the grapes.

The people there were highly introverted,
And seldom spoke when passing through.
I looked for my parents and my grandmother,
But never saw any lost soul that I knew.

The snakes slinked about shy and friendly.
They liked being petted and cuddled warm.
They sang like sparrows instead of hissing—
And bees danced about in a happy swarm.

W. Thomas McQueeney

The bunnies were violent and to be avoided.
They growled and barked like Yorkshire terriers.
The deer that leapt from the thickened reeds
Were from the darkest of devilish areas.

The heaven I thought I thought I knew
Was not bathed in opulence of celestial light.
It was vaguely similar to another dream
Brought on by Jameson's earlier that night.

Trending to a Genre

Categories have subcategories and subsequent sets,
But no one has been able to explain a genre to me yet.
Genres are general, whether made singular or plural.
They're the favorite word of artists, by canvas or mural.

Genres are labels placed upon differing styles of art.
Not related to the subject, the artist, or even the color chart.
Terms invoke the style and the period—like impressionism
Or minimalism, Renaissance, neoclassical, or expressionism.

There's a genre in the sense of literature for review.
Consider fiction, drama, comedy and romance, too.
But a genre can be more than a book or an artful vase—
Genres are used to describe cultures of the human race.

So a genre can be everything, or anything else I suppose—
A genre for films, foods, wines, vehicles, and clothes.
So far as trying to explain or understand genres, I can tell
It makes sense to me there ought to be genre for genres, as well.

Two Irishmen

At half 4:00 a.m., the pub was jammers.
A knackered Irish stuttle was there for craic.
He thought he was jack staggering manky
When a gurrier saw he was heading back.
"He'd lick drink off a scabby leg," he said.
The gouger stook turned hard to the stuttle.
Flutthered himself, he engaged the gobshite
Earning a loud and tenacious rebuttal.
"He has a great lip for the stout," the stuttle told.
"And I sense we'll mill to the dawn accords."
The muck savage stuttle complained in vain,
"I am as sick as a plane to Lourdes."
Just when the stook drew back a hook,
The stuttle loafed him to Smithereens.
A lesson learned is that if you're in a Cork pub,
And ye horse it into ye, be ready by any means.[43]

Averse Again Now and Then

View of Tralee, Ireland, 2007

My Last Dutch Dress
An Amish Girl Leaves the Community for College
(A parody of the poem *My Last Duchess* by Robert Browning[44])

That's my last Dutch dress upon the floor
Looking as if it were an archive. You adore
That dress—no wonder; my bra and pants off to scour,
Easily it lays rumpled there whilst I shower.
Will't please you to sit and look at it. I said,
"Bra and pants off" by design, for I never misread
Strangers like you who measure abstinence
The depth and passion of its yearning glance,
But it's not for myself they return (since none walks by
The shower curtain I have pulled for you; you're shy!)
And I dreamed that they would ask me, in their thirst,
How such a dress fell there; so, you're not the first.
Are you to return and ask thus? Sir, twas not
Your trust and presence only, note that spot
Of corduroy sewn into the Dutch dress sleeve; perhaps
Once the shampoo rinses, and the white towel wraps
With bra and pants off still, flickered embers running warm,
You will leave my Dutch dress alone, and flee my dorm.

Johnny Johnston

Rarely was a man blessed to be as strong
As he was authentic.
Johnny Johnston was square jawed
And chiseled as a god Hellenic.
A hurricane did all it could
To make his home into a pile of wood.

Seventeen loblolly pines lay across his roof
As in a toothpick maze.
Johnny filed his claim and waited
For someone to come for several days.
His wife and children waited too,
Before Johnny decided upon option two.

The area was devastated, no labor,
And a waitlist backlog of people who
Could get to Johnny to remove
Where limbs had broken through—
That's when he decided to protect
His family from a home nearly wrecked.

He called the adjusting firm and got permission
To do the work on his own.
They asked that he keep logbook hours,
So that his work wouldn't be postponed.
They'd pay Johnny a fair hourly amount,
At fifteen dollars if he'd just keep the count.

W. Thomas McQueeney

When the work was complete,
Johnny presented his sheet of fifty hours total.
The adjuster was startled at the high bill
And stated his viewpoint as anecdotal.
"That's an incredible hourly draw
For seventeen trees removed with a chainsaw."

Johnny Johnston was incensed,
An argument commenced—an explanation tendered.
He looked straight ahead, his incredulity unsaid,
His resolve to answer was tempered.
"I worked for six days, the wood piled in stacks,
With no chainsaw at all—I used an axe!"

His claim was paid, and a legend was made
Of the man who chopped away the loblollies.
In the annals of claims, Johnny Johnston's remains
Among the most fantastic of adjusting follies.
He was an honest man and full of life—
His axe saved a fortune over his pocketknife.

My Emoji Is LOL

BTW AFAIK my FB & EM has been hacked.
IMHO some CIA nerd is LHAO, OMG!
TIL my RT is NSFW; IRL hijacked!
FWIW u should LMK if UR the SOB.[45]

Perspective in a Puddle

We should have no ego to coddle or nurse,
As we are but small smidgens in the universe—
And nothing gives us more size paranoia
Than standing next to a California sequoia.

We're smaller yet when our egos inflate—
We're tinier specks and unfettered featherweights.
So why is it that we become so arrogant
Like the flea that thinks he's an elephant?

When we stand alone upon a midnight beach
And see the heavens we'll never reach—
We should be humble, at the height of meekness.
Our strength is that we recognize our weakness.

W. Thomas McQueeney

We're small, we're tiny, the most insignificant dots.
We can elevate humanity by our deeds and our thoughts.
We're destined like toddlers we so long to cuddle—
They're cute and refreshing, but they play in a puddle.

Averse Again Now and Then

First Off at Patriot's Point Golf Course, 2008

Abundant Conundrums

Writers write,
But fingers never fing.
Teachers have taught—
Yet preachers cannot praught.
If something lingers,
It is not a linging.
If you bring something,
When is it brung and not brought?

If one is partially sorry,
Can he make amend?
There's a difference between
Pretend and portend,
In that one is unforeseen.

It takes a ducking
To become a duck.
What do sucklings become?
And since when does it make sense
To ship by truck
Instead of by shipping
Because it would leave a truck dripping.
Was the rhumba invented without rum?
Can thinking too much make the brain numb?

The Throne Drone

Technologies are now upon us.
Higher horizons have been flown.
We built the world's first stealth fighter,
And can buy a personal-use drone.

Can we mix them and make them
Something worthwhile and unique—
That can fly unheard and undetected—
To seek what we do and speak?

I'd have fun steering the stealth drone
And fill it with useful devices,
And fly it in the local mall
To interact with life's little slices.

I'd name the invention the Throne Drone
Because it could parse out God's results—
For every person who shops a mall—
All comers—from children to adults.

I'd arm it with a camera,
A spotlight, and a voice recorder,
A florescent can of spray paint,
And a toy gun full of water.

I'd add a wonderful stockpile
Like diamonds and rich gift cards.
The payload could be delivered
By the most remote of remote regards.

W. Thomas McQueeney

If I'd see a elderly couple
Holding hands while eating lunch,
I'd hover on over to them undetected
To drop diamonds on a hunch.

And if a single mother fretted or sighed,
While searching for coupons to redeem,
I'd lower a dozen enhanced gift cards
To answer her prayers and her dreams.

If thugs loitered to rob the mall—
To shoplift, pickpocket, or loot,
I would spray each culprit with florescence
Helping the cops in their pursuit.

If an agnostic and an atheist
Sat to argue their chosen field.
I'd voice biblical verse from thin air,
And spotlight them as they kneeled.

The toy water gun on my Throne Drone
Would be ready as I listen and watch—
For those who blurt out obscenities—
Each to be squirted in the crotch!

I'd delight in playing God in the mall,
Guiding the stealth quadcopter there within.
But at some point I'd have to realize
The Operator should be Him without sin.

Beauty is an Imperfect Imposter
A Prayer of Perspective

Gifts of the Creator
In rapture of nature
An evening cricket duet
Winter's radiant sunset
The fragrance found in forests
Sparrows and wrens in chorus
Wind waves wheat field crops
Brooks play in watery drops
Butterflies dancing upon thistle
Midnight pulses in a drizzle

We pause, reflect, and gaze
Throughout borrowed days
Inspiration swells
As beauty parallels
The vision of promise
Carried forth in calmness
With patience and kindness
Remind us
What is here and now
Is hundredfold in Your endow

Ruminations
Notes about the content

Nearly six decades ago, my first-grade parochial-school teacher, Sister Mary Redempta, impressed upon me my first sense of the need to promote proper decency. In the following decades, I have often thought back to her influence within the parameters of my parental control rating. Thus, my books have been just a step below what would be considered PG for parental guidance. Even parents are not needed here! I have not written anything that I would be red faced about, should that gentle Catholic nun pick up any of my books. In these times of children's video games that have liberated ratings that parents ignore, I find that a foundation of proper language is both timely and needed in a world gone mad upon vulgarities. Not to be sanctimonious in that regard, I also practice those precepts within my life's meanderings. Language is a classical art not to be impaired by senseless expletives.

There are a few submissions here from many years ago, and others written more recently. Some could be enhanced a bit by explanation. I have attempted to do so "on the spot" by including an endnote where beneficial.

The road map of verse extends from the Conch Republic (Key West) to Seattle, from Maine to San Diego. The states are set in reverse order of their admittance to the United States, starting with Hawaii, the fiftieth state admitted to the Union. They end at Delaware, the first state to sign the U.S. Constitution. They also represent experiences as each has been visited, but not in any particular order. Observances of curiosities and idiosyncrasies are sometimes explored as well as physical features or renowned personalities. The visits were often elongated by a fortunate happenstance such as a festival or a state fair.

Some of the experiences are real, indeed. Other insights are directly from travel experiences, observances, or memorable verbal exchanges. Life, as it unravels, provides such verdant resources. The cultivation is enhanced by the sunshine of the moments. Listen for the inappropriate, the ironic, and the bizarre. Nothing conspires like life itself to support the gift of humor!

Sunrise view of Charleston, 2015

Artwork Notes

All artwork was produced by the author. There is no pretension that the artwork is of any significance, merits a collectible quality, or represents any particular genre or age. It's just paint on canvas for an effect. As in the literature, the author/painter finds no reason to take himself too seriously. In a profound sense, we're all just passing through!

About the Author

A verse Again Now and Then is the fifth book published by author W. Thomas McQueeney. McQueeney is a native of Charleston, South Carolina, and honor graduate of The Citadel with a bachelor of arts degree in English. An active member of the community, he has written over one hundred columns drenched in Carolina Lowcountry humor.

McQueeney serves as the 2017 president of the State of South Carolina Athletic Hall of Fame. He has served as a member of his college trustee board, The Citadel Board of Visitors, and has served other boards, including the St. Francis Xavier Hospital Board of Directors, The Citadel Foundation Board, the Patriot's Point Maritime Foundation, the MUSC Children's Hospital Development Board, and the Board of Directors for Our Lady of Mercy Community Outreach. He chaired the Johnson Hagood Stadium Revitalization project to its conclusion as a $44.5 million enhancement. He chaired the Charleston Metro Sports Council, and the Southern Conference Basketball Championships. He is a Past Grand Knight of Knights of Columbus

Author and light verse poet
W. Thomas McQueeney

Council 704, and past race director of the Knights of Columbus Turkey Day Run, the largest five-thousand-meter running event in South Carolina. He currently serves as chairman of the Medal of Honor Bowl. He has served in similar capacities for myriad community and statewide organizations.

McQueeney is a recipient of the Order of the Palmetto, the state of South Carolina's highest award bestowed upon any citizen. He was inducted into The Citadel Athletic Hall of Fame as an honorary member. He is an accomplished artist, humorist, public speaker, and lecturer. He is one of six brothers who have graduated from The Citadel, a national record for all US military colleges. He is married and has four children and four grandchildren. He resides in Mt. Pleasant, South Carolina, where he operates a small business. In addition to his other avocations, he is an avid traveler, photographer, and historian.

Endnotes

[1] The Sphinx, the yearbook of The Citadel, 1974 edition. Quote from the section dedicated to The Citadel English Department.

[2] Charles Dickens. https://www.brainyquote.com/quotes/authors/c/charles_dickens.html

[3] Algonquin Round Table. Group of humorists who frequented the Algonquin Hotel in New York from 1919-1929. The group included Harpo Marx, Dorothy Parker, and Edna Ferber and two dozen others in the journalism and entertainment businesses. http://www.algonquinroundtable.org/members.html

[4] *A Shropshire Lad*. http://www.shmoop.com/terence-this-is-stupid-stuff/poem-text.html

[5] *Terence, This is Stupid Stuff* from the publication, *A Shropshire Lad*, by Alfred E. Housman (1859-1936). http://www.bartleby.com/123/62.html

[6] Ogden Nash Publications. https://silverbirchpress.wordpress.com/2014/05/17/the-duck-poem-by-ogden-nash/

[7] A Child of the Pluff Mud. Author's self-styled moniker.

[8] Upon Presenting the Laurel. This is written in differing fonts to counterbalance a conversation between the presenter and his conscience. The presenter feels that the award should have been his to receive.

[9] Surely the Tapping Temple. This dance school exists at the location given in the first line of the poem in New York City. The title

is also a reference to the child actress and accomplished tap dancer, Shirley Temple (1928-2014). Shirley Temple Black later served two stints as an appointed U.S. Ambassador.

[10] Each dating site mentioned exists. The preponderance of dating sites has invaded television commercials and the Internet.

[11] Kells. The amazing Book of Kells was visited by the author while in Dublin, Ireland on three occasions.

[12] Edinburgh spelled and Edinburgh said differ. The Scottish city is pronounced as if "Edinborogh," or more succinctly, "Edin-burrah."

[13] Alp Arslan. A storybook warrior from the Seljuk Empire (1029-1072).

[14] Whacko Zack. The poem uses simplicity to contrast the following poem, An Esoteric Sesquipedalian Epitaph, which says the same thing in hard-to-comprehend highbrow overtones.

[15] As described above, this is the antithesis of simplicity. It is the same poem as Whacko Zack, but presented in an academically pretentious manner.

[16] Joan of Arc was a French woman, therefore her name, as heard and written in the French language, would be "Jeanne d'Arc," or pronounced as "John Dark."

[17] The historical use of the word "of" permeates much human history. The denotation is most common to associate a place in lieu of a last name. The word is used three dozen times in the verses presented.

[18] Commodore Mathew C. Perry (1794-1858) lived an incredible worldwide adventure while fathering a house full of children.

[19] Ineffable is defined as too sacred or mighty to be spoken or uttered to others. This unarticulated but lonely subject is like an apparition on a religious level. The thought is that a guardian angel is being watched, but upon inspection, the angel does not materialize and left nothing of richness upon the disappearance.

[20] A villanelle adaptation of Dylan Thomas's famous "Do Not Go Gentle into That Good Night." The villanelle is a rare verse form, and is most associated with this poem.

[21] A giant banyan tree grows near the library in downtown Lahaina on the island of Maui.

[22] In theory, the Americas were settled by nomadic tribes crossing the Bering Sea more than 10,000 years ago. This theory has encountered recent adverse theory from genetic evidence. https://www.scientificamerican.com/article/first-americans-lived-on-bering-land-bridge-for-thousands-of-years/

[23] Oklahoma name derivation. http://www.statesymbolsusa.org/symbol-official-item/oklahoma/state-name-origin/origin-oklahoma

[24] Reporter's question to Roger Miller. http://www.rogermiller.com/bio1.html

[25] "Extinction." Answer given by Roger Miller. http://www.rogermiller.com/memorybook_erick.html

[26] The Fargo, North Dakota, Visitor's Center features a large painted cow statue.

27 Albert Kahn (1869-1942) was a German-born American architect responsible for much of the design of Detroit, Michigan. Importantly, he designed the assembly line for Henry Ford. This innovation made Ford more famous than Kahn. http://architect.architecture.sk/albert-kahn-architect/albert-kahn-architect.php

28 The four-beat meter is odd in poetry, but was used to mirror the simplicity of the architect Albert Kahn's assembly line so that the reader could move through the story faster!

29 Note that this Skakespearean sonnet has the exact meter and rhyme scheme as a standard sonnet of the bard's creation. Also note that each line begins with the poetic letter of the rhyme scheme.

30 The Algonquin nation has many tribes in the American northeast and into Canada.

31 Mississippi facts and notes. http://www.infoplease.com/us-states/mississippi.html

32 Yat, a combination brogue of New Orleans, Louisiana. http://gumbopages.com/yatspeak.html

33 Trial of science teacher John Scopes in Dayton, Tennessee, for teaching evolution. (1925). http://law2.umkc.edu/faculty/projects/ftrials/scopes/evolut.htm

34 Vermont legislature has considered the legalization of marijuana. This has happened in other states. It has become quite controversial in Vermont by 2017. https://www.mpp.org/states/vermont/

35 Discovery and settling of Jamestown. https://www.nps.gov/jame/learn/historyculture/pocahontas-her-life-and-legend.htm

[36] Interstate 95, the main thoroughfare from the Northeast to Florida narrows to two lanes in each direction only in South Carolina.

[37] The state of Connecticut prides itself on the concentration of "haunted" sites listed within the poem.

[38] Delaware allows boat registration without property tax. This legal loophole encourages many yacht owners who do not live in Delaware to register their yachts in the state. http://www.boattax.com/avoid-boat-taxes/

[39] This represents an honest assessment of the author's view of the growing acceptance of verbal vulgarity.

[40] All animals mentioned are native to South America. "Sound" translated, this nonsense verse becomes:

> Two can play down the South American way,
> And I kind of mentioned the chinchilla,
> Taming them as their parent's want us to.
> A capybara's a rat that looks like Godzilla.
>
> I'll pack a llama and you bring a jaguar.
> We'll take her and eat her and maybe sip a slot.
> Okay man, can the weasel try to copy you?
> We hoped to rent to you my car, but got caught.

[41] Sonnet form directs the lines and meter.

[42] Lyrica is a drug produced by Pfizer that has all of the potential side-effects listed in the verse. The drug's television commercials seem to spend more time on the warnings than on the positive impact of a cure.

[43] Irish slang can be quite colorful and differs from Dublin to Cork. The author made ten trips to Ireland and found the slang was rarely vulgar, and sometimes rather humorous and endearing.

[44] Robert Browning (1812-1899) English poet and playwright, famed for the form of the dramatic monologue was considered among the finest of the Victorian poets. The parody is a treatment of *My Last Duchess*. https://www.poetryfoundation.org/poems-and-poets/poems/detail/43768

[45] Texting uses acronyms that minimize the need for typing. "Emojis" give some emphasis by the cartoonish use of facial expressions. http://www.smart-words.org/abbreviations/text.html

Made in the USA
Lexington, KY
15 March 2017